CURRICULUM
ALIGNMENT

Research-Based Strategies for Increasing Student Achievement

DAVID A. SQUIRES

CORWIN PRESS
A SAGE Company

For information:

Corwin Press
A SAGE Company
2455 Teller Road
Thousand Oaks, California 91320
www.corwinpress.com

SAGE Ltd.
1 Oliver's Yard
55 City Road
London, EC1Y 1SP
United Kingdom

SAGE India Pvt. Ltd.
B 1/I 1 Mohan Cooperative
    Industrial Area
Mathura Road, New Delhi 110 044
India

SAGE Asia-Pacific Pte. Ltd.
33 Pekin Street #02–01
Far East Square
Singapore 048763

Printed in the United States of America.

Library of Congress Cataloging-in-Publication Data

Squires, David A.
Curriculum alignment : research-based strategies for increasing
student achievement / David A. Squires.
    p. cm.
Includes bibliographical references and index.
ISBN 978-1-4129-6006-9 (cloth)
ISBN 978-1-4129-6007-6 (pbk.)
  1. Curriculum planning—United States. 2.
Education—Standards—United States. 3. Educational tests and
measurements—United States. 4. Educational accountability—United
States. I. Title.

LB2806.15.S732 2009
375'.001—dc22   2008004873

This book is printed on acid-free paper.

08 09 10 11 10 9 8 7 6 5 4 3 2 1

Acquisitions Editor:	Debra Stollenwerk
Editorial Assistant:	Allison Scott
Production Editor:	Appingo Publishing Services
Cover Designers:	Scott Van Atta
Graphic Designer:	Lisa Riley

CURRICULUM
ALIGNMENT

This book is dedicated to my two daughters,
Allison and Sara, now making their way toward
their own destinies. Allison just received her PhD in
nursing from Yale. Sara is working successfully as a
physical therapist, having received her doctorate from
the University of Southern California.
I am very proud of you both.

Contents

List of What Districts Can Do by Chapter

CHAPTER 2

#2–1 Use Porter's descriptors of instruction in math and science for high school to catalogue what instruction occurs. Align the descriptors with the state test specifications. Confirm that coverage of tested topics improves achievement.

#2–2 Use the Survey of the Enacted Curriculum as a staff development process to compare instruction with standards and state assessments.

#2–3 Rank test results by standards through released test items.

#2–4 Provide teachers with opportunities to refine the scope and sequence of courses (especially for science lecture and lab activities), taking into account problematic areas of standards.

CHAPTER 3

#3–1 Coverage isn't enough—gather data on student practice opportunities in textbooks.

#3–2 Conduct textbook alignment studies keyed to test results.

#6–4 Trim technical vocabulary.

#6–5 Reduce wasteful repetition.

#6–6 Learn to analyze curriculum materials.

#6–7 Align assessment to curriculum.

#6–8 Relate instructional units to strand maps.

#6–9 Create strand maps for other subject areas.

CHAPTER 7

#7–1 Decide on fewer topics covered in more depth, particularly in math.

#7–2 Develop districtwide tests, aligned to state assessments, to gain data on students' mastery of topics.

#7–3 Use test results to vary time and coverage of key topics.

CHAPTER 9

#9–1 Design, write, and implement a curriculum for the district that meets the ten criteria for a useful and usable curriculum.

List of Figures

CHAPTER 4

CHAPTER 5

CHAPTER 6

Preface

In this book I untangle the messy concept of curriculum alignment and use the research as a platform for suggesting ideas a district can use to improve their curriculum, instruction, and test scores.

RATIONALE

I wrote this book with the belief that research, if properly translated, can be a powerful tool in the hands of school and district leaders. Curriculum alignment hasn't benefited from a look at its research base and how it translates into actions districts can take. This book will make an initial contribution.

THE BOOK'S PLAN

I will explain how the concept of alignment has been defined and used:

- in the relationship of alignment to instruction (Chapter 2);
- in a mastery learning setting (Chapter 3);

- for textbooks (Chapter 4);
- in the relationship of standards to standardized tests (Chapter 5);
- in the work of the Third International Math and Science Study (Chapter 6);
- through the work of Project 2061 in science and mathematics (Chapter 7).

Chapter 8 presents an example of a systematic curriculum development approach that incorporates alignment, the Balanced Curriculum. This process for developing and implementing a curriculum uses alignment to strengthen district efforts to improve achievement (Squires, 2005a).

Chapter 9 summarizes the results, showing how a systematic and data-driven approach to curriculum and instruction can address many of the concerns about alignment raised in this book.

The book is divided into three parts.

Part I—Alignment Research and Suggestions Concerning Instruction, Textbooks, and Standardized Tests

This section covers the major areas of concentration in the alignment research:

- a general overview (Chapter 1)
- instruction (Chapter 2)
- textbooks (Chapter 3)
- standardized tests (Chapter 4)

Part II—Alignment Research and Suggestions Concerning Mastery Learning, Project 2061, and the Third International Mathematics and Science Study (TIMSS)

This section moves past the studies concerning just one aspect of the alignment research covered in the book's first part. Part II deals with three examples of a more systematic approach, thus demonstrating that this approach to alignment can also produce achievement results:

- in a mastery learning setting (Chapter 5)
- in Project 2061 in science and mathematics (Chapter 6)
- in the Third International Mathematics and Science Study (Chapter 7)

Part III—The Aligned Curriculum

In Part III, I examine how curriculum is defined, offer ten criteria for a useful and usable curriculum, and model how one curriculum system (the Balanced Curriculum) meets the definition and the criteria, producing improved achievement. A well designed curriculum will produce achievement results.

- Chapters 8 and 9 focus on how alignment can be used in a curriculum design, focusing on the Balanced Curriculum design (Squires, 2005a) as one way of incorporating alignment.
- Chapter 10 summarizes the results of the Balanced Curriculum as one model of alignment, showing improved achievement in districts around the country.
- Chapter 11 summarizes the thirty-one recommendations made in this book based on the research and demonstrates how one curriculum model, the Balanced Curriculum, meets those recommendations.

CHAPTER STRUCTURE

In each chapter I review how researchers have defined, studied, and showed the research-based results of alignment. This review is followed by suggestions of how school districts can use the alignment concept to improve curriculum and instruction.

The focus is on districts because it is the district's responsibility to devise and define a curriculum for its schools. It is too time consuming for schools to do individually.

MY EXPERIENCE

As a district curriculum leader, I have witnessed the power of alignment to strengthen curriculum and drive increased student achievement results (Squires, 2005a). Working with the Comer School Development Program (SDP) at Yale, I have seen student achievement improvements in schools and districts resulting from the combination of the SDP process and an aligned curriculum. Now, as a professor of Educational Leadership at Southern Connecticut State University, I teach students studying to be principals and superintendents by consistently reinforcing the importance of curriculum alignment when they design curriculum structures as part of their course work.

Acknowledgments

A book's author stands on many shoulders.

Many thanks are due the teachers and administrators from the many districts who implemented the Balanced Curriculum process and saw achievement gains. Their skill in developing the curriculum and ensuring implementation shows that a curriculum that accounts for alignment improves achievement.

To the many authors whose work is cited in this book, thanks for your efforts in helping to develop a chorus of studies that show the power of alignment to affect achievement.

To my wife, Maureen, and daughter, Allison, for their many hours of work in reading and commenting on the manuscript. Your love has seen me through this and many other projects.

To three dear friends who also critiqued early versions: Dr. Jim McConnell, Dr. Eileen Howley, and Dr. David Champagne. Your care and your comments inspired further work on my part.

To my editor, Debra Stollenwerk, whose ability to see the logic of the big picture helped me to frame the final draft to fully bring out the book's themes. Your questions, observations, and comments helped me see past my own preconceptions.

PUBLISHER'S ACKNOWLEDGMENTS

Corwin Press gratefully acknowledges the contributions of the following reviewers:

Rosemary Burnett
District Mentor Consultant
School District of La Crosse
La Crosse, WI

About the Author

 **David A. Squires** is currently an associate professor working with doctoral students and teachers who wish to be certified as principals and superintendents in the Educational Leadership Program at Southern Connecticut State University, specializing in curriculum, school reform, and organizational development. Previous employment includes the Comer School Development Program at Yale University. In addition, he has worked as a central office administrator for over a decade in Red Bank, New Jersey; a research specialist at Research for Better Schools in Philadelphia; a graduate research assistant in the Learning Research and Development Center at the University of Pittsburgh; and a high school English teacher in suburban Pittsburgh and inner-city Cleveland. He currently heads a consulting firm, ABC Education Consultants, LLC, which assists school districts to write, align, and implement the Balanced Curriculum process.

About the Balanced Curriculum Web Site

Free access to the Balanced Curriculum Web site can be obtained by visiting the site and, under the log in, clicking on "Free sign up for one course, click here." Directions for using the Web site are given with your free log in.

Professors can receive free access to the Web site for their curriculum courses by emailing david.squires@balancedcurriculum.com and requesting access. Please include the name of your state and the specific standards your students will be aligning to. A syllabus is also available by clicking on "syllabus" from the first page. You can also get the Educational Leadership 685 Curriculum Course description from www.balancedcurriculum.com using login: SCSU Student, password: 1234.

Information is available on the site www.balancedcurriculumcom about the Balanced Curriculum process, services, results, articles, and staff.

To navigate the site, any text in blue can be clicked on to go down to the next level.

By using each of the log ins below, you can view the following sample curricula.

User Name: Demo
Password: Demo

This shows you a number of courses that have been developed by school districts across the country.

User Name: Yale
Password: 1234

This allows you to view student work from graduate students in the Educational Leadership Program at Southern Connecticut State University, where students developed a course with units, one unit of significant tasks, alignments, and assessments.

User Name: Meriden
Teacher Password: 1234

This shows the math curriculum (other curriculum areas are currently under development) for K–5 which produced 10–15% improvement on the Connecticut state test.

User Name: Harvard
Password: 1234

This allows you to view Englewood Cliff, New Jersey, school district's curriculum where all courses have been placed on the Balanced Curriculum Web site.

Part I

Alignment and Instruction, Textbooks, and Standardized Tests

After introducing the concept of alignment and the structure of the research shown in the alignment matrix in Chapter 1, the book's next three chapters summarize major studies in the areas where the majority of the research on alignment is found:

- Instruction (Chapter 2)
- Textbooks (Chapter 3)
- Standardized tests (Chapter 4)

Introduction to Curriculum Alignment

1

Aligning curriculum and instruction to standards and assessments receives much attention from districts that are trying to improve test scores to meet the mandates of No Child Left Behind legislation and requiring ever higher performance on a state's standardized tests. Popular articles from around the world show intensive discussion about the usefulness of alignment (Achieve, Inc., 2001; Ainsworth & Viegut, 2006; Alexson & Kemnitz, 2003; Ananda, 2003; Anderson, 2002 & 2005; Billig et al., 2005; Clarke, Stow, Ruebling, & Kona, 2006; Cronin, 2004; Evans, 2002; Ewing, 2003; Hall, 2002; La Marca, 2001; Lawson, Bordignon, & Nagy, 2002; Marca, Redfield, & Winter, 2001; Maryland State Higher Education Commission, 2004; McGehee & Griffith, 2001; Stern & Roseman, 2001; U.S. Department of Education, 2005). Indeed, research on aligning curriculum with standards and assessments shows dramatic results under some circumstances (Bloom, 1976; Moss-Mitchell, 1998; Porter, Kirst, Osthoff, Smithson, & Schneider, 1994; Price-Baugh, 1997; Schmidt et al., 2001; Squires, 2005a; Squires 2005b; Wishnick, 1989). Many of the studies show that an aligned curriculum can level the playing field for poor and minority students and reduce the achievement gap. Alignment, under some circumstances, produces dramatic results after the first year of implementation, in some cases increasing scores on state testing by over 50% (Squires, 2005a).

Despite the positive effects of alignment on student achievement, little attention is given to alignment issues by many curriculum models, including:

- *Understanding by Design* by Wiggins and McTighe (2005)
- *The Parallel Curriculum* by Tomlinson et al. (2002)
- The Concept-Based Curriculum in *Stiring the Head, Heart, and Soul* by Erickson (2001)
- *Course Design* by Posner and Rudnitsky (2006)
- *Curriculum Mapping* by Jacobs (1997)

Each design has many strengths despite the lack of attention to alignment. Because these popular curriculum designs don't address alignment, however, one powerful dimension of curriculum is lost.

The goal of this book is to refine practitioners' knowledge of alignment issues and to demonstrate what districts can do now to improve their alignment process and student achievement based on the research. The book concludes by demonstrating how curriculum can be a systemic tool for addressing many alignment issues as well as a tool for improving achievement.

This book will appeal to a variety of audiences. Central office personnel in charge of curriculum, staff development, and testing will appreciate the smorgasbord of practical approaches for alignment. Superintendents will use this book as a way to assess their strategies for improving test results and student outcomes. School administrators will use the book to test their approach to alignment against research-based models. Those who are studying curriculum, staff development, assessment, or educational leadership will find the research-based alignment approaches useful in expanding their grab bag of strategies for improving student achievement. School board members, anxious to understand how policy might be constructed to insure continuous improvement in test scores—a dilemma all board members face with the requirements of No Child Left Behind—will appreciate the range of strategies described in the book.

Understanding the concept of alignment is difficult because researchers and school districts use the term *alignment* in many different ways. This book seeks to untangle the messy concept of alignment and use the research as a platform for suggesting ideas a district can use to improve their curriculum, instruction, and test scores.

WHAT IS ALIGNMENT?

Alignment is an agreement or a match between two categories. If standards contain "number concepts" in math and the curriculum contains "number concepts," alignment between standards and curriculum occurs. The categories match. In this example, the alignment presupposes that the contents of "number concepts" are the same for both the standards and the curriculum.

Standards can be aligned to curriculum. Standards are general; curriculum is more specific. For example, in a writing standard is the description, "Write on self-selected topics in a variety of literary forms." The curriculum contains a number of specific writing opportunities for students to write on self-selected topics in a variety of specific literary forms. Each writing opportunity so specified is aligned to the standard, and the curriculum and the standards match, or are in alignment, even though the standards are general and the curriculum specific. Ensuring alignment means that students will have the opportunity to learn the content of the standards.

The process of alignment becomes difficult when we examine the number of documents that could be aligned and compared. Figure 1.1 has two columns that list the major areas that could be aligned or compared. Arrows

Figure 1.1   Alignment Possibilities

National Standards From Professional Organizations	National Standards From Professional Organizations
NAEP, SAT, ACT	NAEP, SAT, ACT
Commercial Standardized Tests	Commercial Standardized Tests
State Standards	State Standards
State Assessments	State Assessments
Textbooks	Textbooks
District Curriculum	District Curriculum
District Standards	District Standards
District Assessments	District Assessments
Teacher Lesson Plans	Teacher Lesson Plans
Teacher Assessment	Teacher Assessment
Teacher Instruction	Teacher Instruction
Teacher Assignments	Teacher Assignments

SOURCE: (Squires, 2005a)

beginning in the first column show that national standards from professional organizations can be aligned to the categories in the second column. (All the possible arrows are not shown in this example.) Alignment can be a daunting task because there are so many possible alignments.

We wish national standards would align with state standards and state standards would align with local standards. We wish national tests such as the NAEP, SAT, and ACT would align with commercial standardized tests, state assessments, district, and teacher assessments. We wish that textbooks, district curriculum, and teacher lesson plans would align with teacher instruction. What we wish and what we know are different.

ALIGNMENT PROBLEMS: TOO MANY STANDARDS, TOO LITTLE TIME

What we know is that any category in Figure 1.1 listed above District Curriculum has been created in relative isolation from all the others. Commercial tests may not reflect many state standards. State assessments may not be aligned to textbooks. The standards of national professional associations may have little relationship to the NAEP, SAT, or ACT. As we work in a standards-based world, we find the tools we work with are not aligned.

Consider the many layers of standards: state standards drive state assessment specifications, national standards inform state standards, and districts may have developed ways of working on their own—their own "power" standards (Reeves, 2006). The voluminous nature of state standards guarantees that no one can keep all the standards in his or her head at once, especially if one is in a self-contained elementary classroom responsible for math, English/language arts, social studies, and science. There are not enough hours in a day to ensure that students will individually perform on all those standards. Do we have a way of selecting the most important?

Yes! A district's curriculum defines a plan for what is most important for students to know and be able to do. A local district can control their curriculum assessments, and thus can direct teacher lesson plans, instruction, and assessments. The district curriculum is the meeting place for all those voices of state and national entities, and district teachers can decide what's best for their students based on their professional judgment and expertise, the standards, the textbooks, and the tests. Once the district curriculum is developed, alignment to the many competing standards and assessments with which districts must cope can take place. Then it is possible to see if there is over- or under-alignment between the curriculum, the textbooks, state and national standards and assessments, and other areas such as college entrance tests like the ACT or SAT. (Many of you are shuddering right now because you know your district's curriculum, in its current form, is not up to such a task. The curriculum model shown in the last chapter is one way to address this issue.)

There is an advantage to the many voices from standards and local practice telling us what is important for students to know and do, but it is personnel at the district level who must decide what should be taught in the district. These many voices of standards and assessments can help inform decisions about what is most important to teach. A district curriculum provides a way to make decisions locally about what is most important to teach and test. Then the district can determine whether the curriculum is strong by aligning the curriculum to external standards and assessments and seeing where the gaps are or what is overemphasized. If your curriculum can't do this easily, your district is missing an important lever to improve student achievement.

Here's a vision of what can happen when alignment is in place. Webb (1997) indicates that teachers will give more importance to documents if alignment exists because the documents will be more useful in teaching students. Alignment can improve the effectiveness and efficiency of the school system by providing feedback on standards that need more work, so money and time can be allocated based on need. Improving scores on state assessments reinforce what is taught and learned. In an aligned system, student progress is more easily mapped through large-scale assessments and district- or teacher-made assessments that parallel the large-scale assessments. Professional development, textbook adoption, and budgeting processes can be increasingly driven by student results. Results of the research on alignment summarized in this book show that student performance is better when alignment is in place.

Districts that naïvely trod into alignment territory will immediately hit a quagmire of competing standards and assessments. This book provides a way to know what the research says about alignment, so the district can develop strategies to align their curriculum and thus improve student achievement. To assist in sorting out the research, let's use the alignment matrix.

THE ALIGNMENT MATRIX

English's three components of curriculum—the written, the taught, the tested (English, 1992)—provide a first cut in examining the problem of alignment. The written curriculum is usually the curriculum document produced by the school district. Textbooks also are another form of written curriculum. Another form of written curriculum is the standards. Standards, curriculum, and textbooks are three areas addressed in the written section of the curriculum matrix.

The taught curriculum comes from enacting the written curriculum. The taught curriculum on the curriculum matrix consists of two categories: lesson plans which teachers use to plan what they teach and actual classroom instruction.

The tested curriculum is the relatively small part of the curriculum that ends up on a test. The tested curriculum is the content that is tested within the school district in curriculum embedded tests, or the content of state or other standardized tests. The curriculum matrix divides the tested curriculum into state and standardized tests (the most general), curriculum embedded tests, and student assignments. (Student assignments can be considered test-like as they are used by teachers as indicators that students have understood the material.)

Any of these categories can be aligned to any of the other categories, with complete alignment shown in Figure 1.2 (Squires, 2005a). The research covers most of these alignment possibilities (see Chapter 9 for a summary of the alignment research placed on the alignment matrix).

We will use the alignment matrix to organize our literature review and summarize the various ways that researchers have studied curriculum alignment. For each literature review section, the alignment categories are connected on the alignment matrix for the research cited.

The next chapter discusses the alignment research around instruction and suggests a few ways districts might use that information to improve alignment.

Figure 1.2   The Alignment Matrix

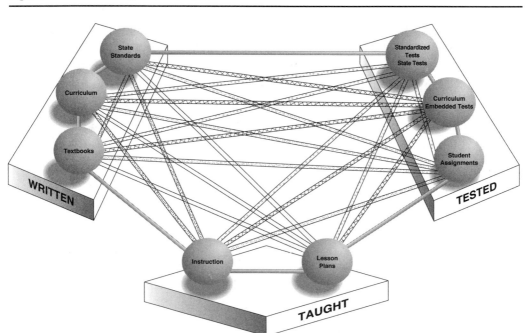

Alignment and Instruction

This chapter reviews the research on aligning curriculum to instruction. What happens in the classroom influences all other aspects of alignment; so we begin looking at the alignment research that focuses on instruction. In the chapter's first section, Porter's work examines a way to categorize the content of science in high school science classes, compares this with other classes, and shows the effect of content coverage on achievement gains. In the second section, these ideas are extended to large school districts to see if similar tools can be applied to improve the alignment of instruction, standards, and state tests. In the third section of the chapter, we review three studies that show how alignment considerations have been integrated into school improvement and curriculum development processes, with some improvements in achievement noted. At the end of the chapter, we show how school districts can use similar processes to improve alignment of instruction.

THE REFORM UP CLOSE STUDY AND ALIGNMENT'S DIMENSIONS

Reform Up Close Study—Purpose and Approach

Porter and colleagues, in the Reform Up Close project (1993, 1994), studied high schools (two each in large urban districts and one in a smaller suburban/rural district) in six states that were actively implementing change in curriculum and instruction in math and science, such as increased course requirements and more emphasis on problem solving. The high schools, as part of increasing state requirements, generally required more students to take higher-level courses. For example, some of the high schools eliminated general math and required all students to take Algebra I. The study reported on whether the enacted (taught) curriculum in math and science courses were watered down as a result of increased enrollments. This required an "alignment" of course content mapped from the "old" to the "new" courses to determine if there was a difference between the old course and the new course.

To describe the enacted (taught) curriculum across schools, they employed a set of descriptors for math and science topics covered in each classroom to focus the alignment effort.

In the Reform Up Close study, we employed a detailed and conceptually rich set of descriptors of high school mathematics and science that were organized into three dimensions: *topic coverage*, *cognitive demand*, and *mode of presentation*. Each dimension consisted of a set number of discrete descriptors. *Topic coverage* consisted of 94 distinct categories for mathematics (for example, ratio, volume, expressions, and relations between operations). *Cognitive demand* included nine descriptors: memorize, understand concepts, collect data, order/compare/estimate, perform procedures, solve routine problems, interpret data, solve novel problems, and build/revise proofs. There were seven descriptors for *modes of presentation*: exposition, pictorial models, concrete models, equations/formulas, graphical, laboratory work, and fieldwork. A content topic was defined as the intersection of *topic coverage*, *cognitive demand*, and *mode of presentation*, so the language permitted $94 \times 9 \times 7$ or 5,922 possible combinations for describing content. Each lesson could be described using up to five unique three-dimensional topics, yielding an extremely rich yet systematic language for describing instructional content. This language worked well for daily teacher logs and for observation protocols (Porter & Smithson, 2001, p. 5).

Porter used the same three dimensions in describing daily teacher logs (lesson plans on the alignment matrix), teacher survey instruments of what teachers said they taught (instruction on the alignment matrix), and the topic coverage dimension for aligning lessons to emerging national standards (standards on the alignment matrix). This method allows for comparison or alignment between instruction, teacher plans, and standards.

Findings

In general, the daily teacher logs, the teacher questionnaire, and the observation protocols aligned in that all descriptions were consistent with each other; they all described, in different ways, the classroom instruction. (The researchers wouldn't want the teacher observation protocols to differ from what the teachers recorded in their daily logs.) Use of the chart defining the intersection of topic coverage, cognitive demand, and mode of presentation described above provided a quick way to summarize and describe the content of lessons. Porter's approach of constructing a chart of content topics allowed comparison across states with different state standards for describing math and science. Having a universal way to describe instruction provides common data points for research, linking instruction to achievement outcomes and internal district evaluation activities. (A similar approach was taken in the Third International Mathematics and Science Study, which we will review in Chapter 7.)

Porter found that "content of mathematics and science courses appeared not to have been compromised by increased enrollments (in more difficult courses); and the enacted curriculum in high school mathematics and science was not at all in alignment with the curriculum reform toward higher-order thinking and problem-solving for all students" (Porter et al., 1994, p.8). Additionally, Porter noted

> We were able to demonstrate a strong, positive, and significant correlation (.49) between the content of instruction and student achievement gains. When we controlled for prior achievement, students' poverty level, and content of instruction (using an HLM [Hierarchical Linear Modeling] approach in our analysis), practically all variation in student learning gains among types of first-year high school mathematics courses was explained (Porter et al., 1994, p. 4).

The power of alignment is demonstrated, this time showing that aligned instruction is linked to increased student outcomes (Gamoran, Porter, Smithson & White, 1997). This is shown on the alignment matrix (Figure 2.1) shown next.

At the bottom of the alignment matrix, the three studies listed in this section are labeled with an A. The A indicates that each study looked at the alignment of lesson plans with student data. Other alignment relationships were also investigated in these three studies: the alignment between instruction and lesson plans, the alignment between curriculum and instruction, and the alignment of instruction to standards. Each is indicated by an A with a line connecting the alignment categories.

Figure 2.1   The Alignment Matrix

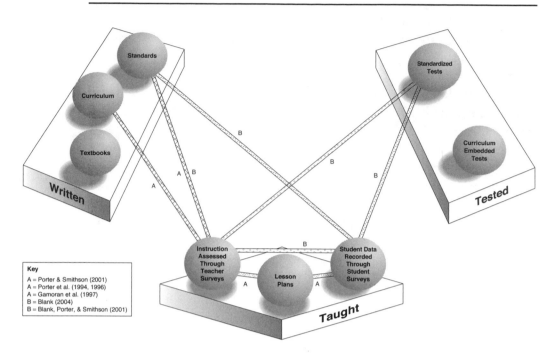

Next we will explain other studies by Blank (2004) and Blank, Porter, and Smithson (2001), showing relationships between other alignment categories related to instruction indicated by the letter *B* in Figure 2.1. At the book's end, all the studies will be shown on one alignment matrix so the reader will be able to visualize the total scope of the research. (See Chapter 10.)

INSTRUCTIONAL ALIGNMENT AND PROFESSIONAL DEVELOPMENT

In "New Tools for Analyzing Teaching, Curriculum and Standards in Mathematics and Science," Blank, Porter, and Smithson (2001) developed tools for data reporting on a number of alignment categories summarized before on the alignment matrix. Then they tried to get large school districts to apply their findings through professional development.

Blank et al.: *Refining Data Gathering and Procedures for Alignment—Purpose and Approach*

Blank et al. (2001) methodology builds on the findings of Porter's studies. Rather than record the cognitive demand and mode of presentation for each lesson on a three-dimensional matrix, teachers filled out a one-time survey highlighting content, cognitive demand, and an estimate of how long they spent on a particular topic for an entire year, recorded in a survey of the enacted curriculum shown in Figure 2.2.

The first column of the survey asks teachers to indicate the amount of time on topic. The second column asks teachers to indicate the subtopics for

Figure 2.2   Survey of the Enacted Curriculum

Sample Sections from Survey

Subject Content: Mathematics

Time on Topic	Middle School Mathematics Topics	Expectations for Students in Mathematics					
<none>	Number Sense/ Properties	Memorize	Understand Concepts	Perform Procedures	Analyze/ Reason	Solve Novel Problems	Integrate
⓪ ① ② ③	Place value	⓪ ① ② ③	⓪ ① ② ③	⓪ ① ② ③	⓪ ① ② ③	⓪ ① ② ③	⓪ ① ② ③
⓪ ① ② ③	Whole numbers	⓪ ① ② ③	⓪ ① ② ③	⓪ ① ② ③	⓪ ① ② ③	⓪ ① ② ③	⓪ ① ② ③
⓪ ① ② ③	Operations	⓪ ① ② ③	⓪ ① ② ③	⓪ ① ② ③	⓪ ① ② ③	⓪ ① ② ③	⓪ ① ② ③
⓪ ① ② ③	Fractions	⓪ ① ② ③	⓪ ① ② ③	⓪ ① ② ③	⓪ ① ② ③	⓪ ① ② ③	⓪ ① ② ③
⓪ ① ② ③	Decimals	⓪ ① ② ③	⓪ ① ② ③	⓪ ① ② ③	⓪ ① ② ③	⓪ ① ② ③	⓪ ① ② ③
⓪ ① ② ③	Percents	⓪ ① ② ③	⓪ ① ② ③	⓪ ① ② ③	⓪ ① ② ③	⓪ ① ② ③	⓪ ① ② ③
⓪ ① ② ③	Ratio, proportion	⓪ ① ② ③	⓪ ① ② ③	⓪ ① ② ③	⓪ ① ② ③	⓪ ① ② ③	⓪ ① ② ③
⓪ ① ② ③	Patterns	⓪ ① ② ③	⓪ ① ② ③	⓪ ① ② ③	⓪ ① ② ③	⓪ ① ② ③	⓪ ① ② ③
⓪ ① ② ③	Real numbers	⓪ ① ② ③	⓪ ① ② ③	⓪ ① ② ③	⓪ ① ② ③	⓪ ① ② ③	⓪ ① ② ③
⓪ ① ② ③	Exponents, scientific notation	⓪ ① ② ③	⓪ ① ② ③	⓪ ① ② ③	⓪ ① ② ③	⓪ ① ② ③	⓪ ① ② ③
⓪ ① ② ③	Factors, multiples, divisibility	⓪ ① ② ③	⓪ ① ② ③	⓪ ① ② ③	⓪ ① ② ③	⓪ ① ② ③	⓪ ① ② ③

INSTRUCTIONAL ACTIVITIES IN MATHEMATICS

Listed below are some questions about what students in the target class do in mathematics. For each activity, pick one of the choices (0, 1, 2, 3) to indicate the percentage of instructional time that students are doing each activity. Please think of an average student in this class when responding.

What percentage of mathematics instructional time in the target class do students:

NOTE: No more than two 3's, or four 2's should be reported for this set of items.

		None	Less than 25%	25% to 33%	More than 33%
34	Watch the teacher demonstrate how to do a procedure or solve a problem.	⓪	①	②	③
35	Read about mathematics in books, magazines, or articles.	⓪	①	②	③
36	Collect or analyze data.	⓪	①	②	③
37	Maintain and reflect on a mathematics portfolio of their own work.	⓪	①	②	③
38	Use hands-on materials or manipulatives (e.g., counting blocks, geometric shapes, algebraic tiles).	⓪	①	②	③
39	Engage in mathematical problem solving (e.g., computation, story-problems, mathematical investigations).	⓪	①	②	③
40	Take notes.	⓪	①	②	③
41	Work in pairs or small groups (non-laboratory).	⓪	①	②	③
42	Do a mathematics activity with the class **outside** the classroom.	⓪	①	②	③
43	Use computers, calculators, or other technology to learn mathematics.	⓪	①	②	③
44	Work individually on assignments.	⓪	①	②	③
45	Take a quiz or test.	⓪	①	②	③

the content covered, such as Number Sense/Properties. In the other columns teachers indicate time use categories: 0 = no emphasis, 1 = slight emphasis [accounts for less than 25% of the time], 2 = moderate emphasis [accounts for 25–33% of the time], 3 = sustained emphasis [accounts for more than 33% of the time] (Council of Chief State School Officers, 2000; Porter & Smithson, 2001). The categories of cognitive demand have also been refined over time (Porter & Smithson, 2001). The survey shown in the second chart in Figure 2.2 collects data on the amount of time spent on various instructional activities. Porter and Smithson showed that the abbreviated data collection method correlated well with the daily instructional surveys used in Reform Up Close work. Data from student questionnaires allowed a comparison between student and teacher questionnaires with adequate correlations indicating reliability. The survey of the enacted curriculum reduces the data collection demands of alignment to once per year, from recording alignment for every lesson as in the Reform Up Close effort.

The teacher questionnaires and the analysis of state standards and state tests across eleven states allowed rich comparisons with the authors providing suggestions about how the data might be used by states, districts, and schools, such as:

- to examine main differences in practices among schools and teachers
- to compare current instruction to standards
- to analyze subject content taught in a topic area
- to compare schools within and across districts
- to align between instruction and assessment

Below is a sample of the reports showing data from the questionnaires.

Findings

Figure 2.3 shows an alignment analysis of Grade 8 NAEP (National Assessment of Educational Progress) assessment with a state assessment and with a state teachers' report summarizing the average of fourteen teachers' questionnaire results showing their curriculum coverage. The shaded topographical representation indicates the time spent on the intersection of content (Nature of Science, Measurement and Calculation in Science, etc.) with cognitive demand (memorize, understand concepts, etc.). For example, the NAEP chart indicates that the test topic for Life Science requires students to answer questions involving memorization on approximately 9+% of the test's content. On the other hand, teachers from state B report spending 3–4.9% of their time on Life Science memorization.

Figure 2.3   Alignment Analysis of State Assessments, Teacher Reports, and NAEP Assessment

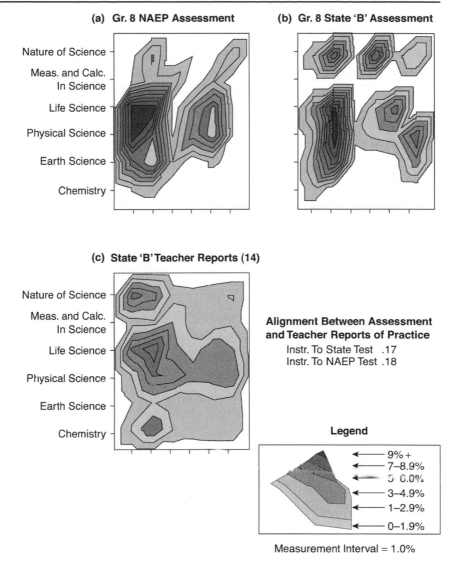

SOURCE: Porter, A. C., & Smithson J. L. (2001). *Defining, developing, and using curriculum indicators* (CPRE Research Report Series RR-048). Philadelphia: Consortium for Policy Research in Education, University of Pennsylvania.

Teachers would need to figure out whether their instruction on Life Science memorization provided enough time to produce adequate scores on the NAEP in items that involved Life Science memorization. Further discussion can be obtained in Porter and Smithson's paper entitled "Alignment of assessments, standards, and instruction using curriculum indicator data" (2002). This report provides specific documentation on ways data from teacher surveys of alignment can be used to change policy and school and district practices.

Blank: Applying Alignment Strategies in Urban Settings—Purpose and Approach

Can and will the data be used by teachers and administrators in real-world settings? Here the authors are interested in the tool's use in staff development. Could the tool be used by teachers to inform their decisions about curriculum and instruction? Here alignment is moving away from a research tool and evolving into a staff development tool.

To begin to answer this question, the Council of Chief State School Officers was awarded a three-year grant from the National Science Foundation (NSF) in 2000 to conduct an experimental design study to determine the effectiveness of a new model for professional development, which aimed toward improving the quality of instruction in math and science in five urban districts, with a total of forty middle schools comprising the pool for random selection of the groups. A professional development model (Council of Chief State School Officers, 2002) was synthesized using research on staff development.

Four elements were part of the design:

- active learning opportunities for teachers, responsive to how teachers learn and take leadership roles
- extended duration sustained over time
- focus on content, high standards, and how students learn the content
- collective participation of groups of teachers from the same school or department (Blank, 2004, p. 6)

"To provide effective formative evaluation designed to improve quality of curriculum and instruction requires reliable, comparable data that allows educators to determine the degree of consistency in the curriculum being taught, and then to identify the source of variation in the enacted curriculum, the subject content, and classroom practices" (Blank, 2002; Porter, 2002) [quoted from Blank, 2004, p. 6]. The school teams had three goals:

- learn to use rich, in-depth data to inform decisions about curriculum, practice, assessment, organization, and materials
- gain skills in collecting, analyzing, and displaying data; working collaboratively; and organizing data-driven dialogue
- learn how to set measurable student learning goals; develop data-driven, local improvement plans; and sustain processes

Teachers in the control schools received inservice training on how to use the data on the enacted curriculum.

Steps in the Assistance Model Process

Year 1

Orientation of district and school leaders: teachers complete baseline data

Introductory Professional Development Workshop 1 for leader teams (two days): develop data skills and begin data inquiry

Technical assistance in schools to introduce model to teachers

Year 2

Professional Development Workshop 2 (one day): use of content data and instructional practices data

Technical assistance in schools

Professional Development Workshop 3 (one day): analyzing student work and comparing instructional strategies

Technical assistance in schools

Refocus efforts within schools

Year 3

Continue school teamwork

Complete follow-up surveys with teachers

SOURCE: (Blank, 2004, p. 11)

In three districts the study's authors encountered problems at the central office level getting schools identified and maintaining a commitment to the study's goals and processes. Change in district leadership with consequent change in priorities was also a problem. Teacher mobility was a problem. "Of the 660 math and science teachers (treatment and control) in study schools in year 1, only 49 % were in the same school and subject assignment in year 3" (Blank, 2004, p. 72). And, "Only one-fourth of the teachers in the study who completed the baseline teacher survey in year 1 also completed the follow-up teacher survey in year 3" (Blank, 2004, p. 56). Therefore, conclusions reached from the study contain only a small set of teachers who were in the same assignment, participated in the staff development, and filled out the pre-post surveys.

Findings

For those with complete data, there were two findings. First, the data on enacted curriculum (DEC) model did improve quality of instruction, as measured by increasing alignment with state standards, when comparing instruction in treatment schools with control schools; however, the effects are contingent on the level and effectiveness of implementation within the treatment schools. This means that schools may have paid attention to alignment, but they were only effective if the decisions about alignment were implemented in classroom instruction.

Second, schools with a high level of participation in DEC activities showed greater increases in alignment of instructional content with state standards than did other schools (Blank, 2004, p. 56). A description of current resources, materials, and processes available for local districts and state departments can be found in the Council of Chief State School Officers' Surveys of Enacted Curriculum (2005).

The works of Porter and Smithson and Blank show the wonderful possibilities in aligning curriculum with valid and reliable instruments and also show the difficulty of getting the instruments used in the real world to help teachers and administrators make a difference in instruction for children. Although this work could be used to describe curriculum, just as the Surveys of the Enacted Curriculum can show the alignment with state standards and assessments, the enacted curriculum focuses on instruction and individual teachers' reporting of their instructional emphasis. Further, the enacted curriculum assumes (perhaps rightly so) that districts don't have a way of controlling what teachers teach and test, such as a district curriculum. The enacted curriculum model does place emphasis on the "intended curriculum," but the intended curriculum is quickly equated to state standards.

The authors of the enacted curriculum have missed an intervening variable in their model—the district curriculum. Perhaps this is because many districts have never seen a district curriculum that makes a difference in student achievement or is powerful enough to actually provide direction to district teachers on what is most important to teach and test. Squires (2005a) has developed a Web-based curriculum development process that aligns the curriculum to state standards and state and nationally normed assessments. It provides standardized ways to assess the curriculum, so data is generated for continuing improvement of the curriculum and the curriculum completion can be managed and administrated electronically. We address this curriculum model in more detail in Chapters 8 and 9 of this book.

THREE SMALLER STUDIES OF INSTRUCTIONAL ALIGNMENT

In this section we review three studies that show how alignment considerations have been integrated into school improvement and curriculum development processes. Although limited in scope, the next three studies show that the concept of alignment influences thinking on how to improve in the instructional domain. McGehee and Griffith (2001) report on a staff development process for faculties to examine and understand the alignment between state tests and instruction for students. DiBiase, Warren, and Wagner (2002) demonstrate the process of alignment of instruction to standards and assessment, resulting in better student achievement. These studies are placed on the alignment matrix in Figure 2.4.

Understanding the Alignment Between State Tests and Instruction—Purpose and Approach

McGehee and Griffith (2001) developed a process that can be used with school or district staff to assist them in understanding the content of the state and/or standardized tests and their implications for instruction. The activity involves released items from state or standardized tests.

The activity involves printing each released item, including the open-response items, in large print on color-coded cards. The colors indicate one of the five content strands (for the state standards of Arkansas). K–4 teachers and 5–8 teachers are divided into two groups for each benchmarking level. Each group is given a set of cards and the ranking of the 45 test items determined by the percentage correct for that school or district. One group is asked to sort the cards from lowest percentage item to highest percentage

Figure 2.4   The Alignment Matrix—Focus on Instruction

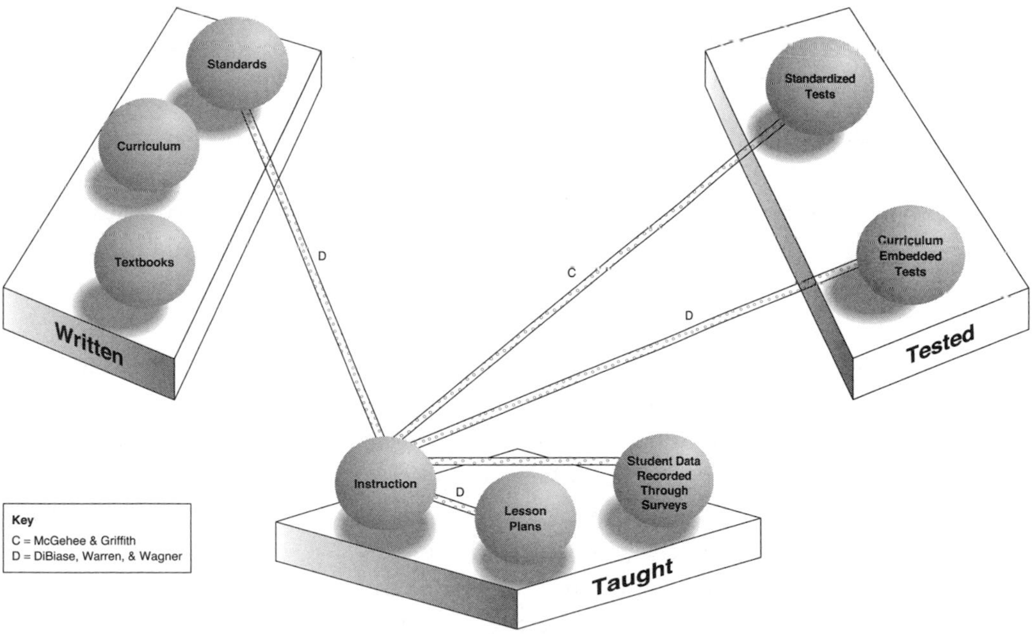

Key
C = McGehee & Griffith
D = DiBiase, Warren, & Wagner

item and to divide this sort into quartiles (the highest 12, the next best 11, the next 11, the lowest 11). The other benchmarking level group is asked to sort the cards by strands and within each strand, then, sort the cards from best to worse. The whole group assembles around each sort starting with the quartile sort for the fourth grade benchmark exam and ending with the strand sort for the eighth grade benchmark. (McGehee & Griffith, 2001, p. 141)

Teacher groups then discuss the implications these sorts have for instruction. The authors reported that groups discussed computation, classroom materials like work sheets versus hands-on problem solving, and the roles of textbooks in the curriculum. This leads to a discussion and consensus on a scope and sequence for curriculum and instruction.

Findings

The authors reported results showing that a small northeastern Arkansas district increased each of its Stanford Achievement Tests: nine percentile points for fourth grade and at least 10 points for eighth grade. Another district in western Arkansas advanced to 72 % of their students gaining proficiency on state tests compared with 37 % proficient as a statewide average. Further research in other districts will be forthcoming. Such results indicate that if teachers have the information—and if they can apply the information to instruction—then it is possible to improve student achievement.

Aligning Laboratory Instruction With Lectures—Purpose and Approach

DiBiase, Warren, and Wagner (2002) aligned the instruction in a chemistry lecture at the college level, meeting three times a week, with the instruction of a chemistry laboratory course meeting once a week. The goal of this project was to develop a laboratory curriculum and instruction that aligned intimately with the lecture and also used some of the principles of the National Science Education Standards (curriculum-standards alignment). Using content analysis procedures, the authors found that ten of the fourteen labs were not linked in scheduling to the topics discussed in the lecture. They adopted an instructional model that consisted of pre-assessment, exploration, concept development, concept application, and assessment to reinforce the inquiry-based nature of the curriculum. Students at the beginning of the course were randomly assigned to experimental and control groups; the experimental group was given instruction that aligned the lab with the lectures, the control group was given the former sequence of instruction. At the end of the course all students took the same exam. Data was gathered about students' background through a pre-semester assessment delving into previous science and mathematics courses taken and students' SAT scores. They also collected opinion surveys administered halfway through the semester. Randomly selected students were interviewed to ascertain the effectiveness of course design on student achievement. All the laboratory instructors also were interviewed.

Findings

There were no statistically significant differences between the experimental and control groups before the instruction commenced, based on pre-semester assessment delving into previous science and mathematics courses and SAT scores. There was a significant increase in the final test scores for the course in the experimental sections. Based on the lab surveys presented at mid-semester, students in the experimental group believed that there was a tight connection between the lecture and the lab experiments that helped them understand the lecture: the students understood (rather than just memorized) the concepts and calculations, and the experiments helped them to visualize the concepts and processes from the lecture. From the students interviewed, most students in the control group noted the deficiencies in the curriculum, while most in the experimental group commented positively about their experiences.

Taking the studies in this section, as a whole, we see that beginning with instructional concerns doesn't preclude a necessity to align instruction to a scope and sequence of a course, as in the DiBiase, Warner, and Wagner (2002) study. Many staff development alternatives can help focus teachers on standards and assessments, as was shown with the McGehee and Griffith (2001) study.

WHAT DISTRICTS CAN DO

#2–1

Use Porter's descriptors of instruction in math and science for high school to catalogue what instruction occurs. Align the descriptors with the state test specifications. Confirm that coverage of tested topics improves achievement.

For example, if all teachers were doing a lesson on ratio, they could then fill in the matrix in Figure 2.5 indicating the appropriate categories of cognitive demand and modes of presentation.

Figure 2.5   Porter's Descriptors for Math and Science Applied to Ratio

	Memorize	Understand Concepts	Collect Data	Order/ Compare/ Estimate	Perform Procedures	Solve Routine Problems	Interpret Data	Solve Novel Problems	Build/ Revise Proofs
Exposition									
Pictorial Models									
Concrete Models									
Equations/ Formulas									
Graphical									
Lab Work									
Field Work									

Teachers would make an *X* in the matrix showing how concept of ratio was taught. Then they would compare how they taught ratio with how ratio was presented in the state standards and how the item was assessed by the state assessment.

Samples of the state standards and state assessment from Connecticut are shown in Figures 2.6 and 2.7, respectively.

Pluses

- Porter's descriptors have proven to be valid and reliable and useful in comparisons of what has been presented in classrooms.
- Examining coverage of topics has been shown to affect achievement in math and science.

Figure 2.6   Connecticut Standards for Number Properties

2.2 Use numbers and their properties to compute flexibly and fluently, and to reasonably estimate measures and quantities.	b. Solve proportional reasoning problems.	**(1)** Use dimensional analysis to determine equivalent rates. **(2)** Solve problems using direct and inverse variation.

SOURCE: Connecticut Mastery Test Third Generation Mathematics Handbook, Part 1, Connecticut State Department of Education, 1999.

Figure 2.7   Sample Performance Item for the Connecticut State Test

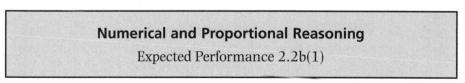

Numerical and Proportional Reasoning
Expected Performance 2.2b(1)

Maple Syrup – GI

To make maple syrup, Ken must boil 40 gallons of maple tree sap to produce one gallon of syrup. Ken sells his maple syrup in containers that hold 1 quart. At that rate, how many **gallons** of maple tree sap must be boiled to make 1 quart of syrup?

SOURCE: Connecticut Mastery Test Third Generation Mathematics Handbook, Part 1, Connecticut State Department of Education, 1999.

Other Considerations

- Because there are 94 topic areas for mathematics in Porter's matrix, 94 pages would need to be filled out.

Teachers need time to become familiar with the coding system and to fill out the necessary forms on a daily basis. (In the next section of this chapter, Porter shows a valid and reliable way to gather information on a yearly basis rather than a daily basis.)

#2–2

Use the Survey of the Enacted Curriculum as a staff development process to compare instruction with standards and state assessments.

The Survey of the Enacted Curriculum provides a way to have data-based decision making on curricular issues founded upon a research-based, valid, and reliable instrument. Numerous comparisons are possible: teacher to teacher, school to school, teacher, school, or district to state assessment results and/or state standards.

Pluses

- This valid and reliable instrument provides the data-based decisions that can be aggregated by teacher, school, and district to provide many different comparisons between the taught and tested curriculum and the written curriculum encompassed in the state standards.

Other Considerations

- The model does not assume a written curriculum, but assumes that the written curriculum is the state standards. Instruction among individual teachers and schools can be compared, but there is no vehicle for comparing instruction with a district curriculum. This model assumes that the analysis of an individual teacher's ways of instruction will be powerful enough to distinguish a one best model of a course's design. Given the problems that districts had in using the results, including high rates of teacher turnover and lack of central office commitment, it may be unrealistic that a one best way can bubble up through the data in most districts.

#2–3

Rank test results by standards through released test items.

Districts can mimic the processes described by McGehee and Griffith (2001), coding the released test items by standards, then having a school's faculty sort them and discuss the implications for instruction.

Pluses

- Once the coding is accomplished, this method provides a sophisticated look at the results.
- Faculty discussions have been shown to result in gains on standardized tests.

Other Considerations

- The conversations are disconnected from a written curriculum. (Indeed, in the article no written district curriculum was mentioned.) But then we are examining alignment research around instruction.
- If a curriculum was present, and multiple schools used the curriculum, a district would need to develop a way to synthesize the recommendation of each school's faculties.

#2–4

Provide teachers with opportunities to refine the scope and sequence of courses (especially for science lecture and lab activities), taking into account problematic areas of standards.

The DiBiase, Warren, and Wagner (2002) study points out that elaborate alignment strategies may not be necessary in order to affect course performance; rather, careful work on sequencing and coordinating topics around science themes, and appropriately organizing instruction, can pay dividends in student achievement.

Pluses

- Attending to instructional design to improve the alignment between course modules and standards pays dividends in student achievement.

Other Considerations

- Institutionalize the work, by writing it down and having others use it, in order to capture the gains for future students.

Alignment
and Textbooks

This chapter focuses on alignment of textbooks to the curriculum categories on the alignment matrix. Readers will know what the research says about textbook alignment and what research-based strategies can be used for improving the use textbooks.

In many districts, textbooks primarily guide instruction. The district presents teachers with textbooks and expects them to teach the textbook's content. The textbooks in this case are fulfilling the function of curriculum, providing a structure so teachers can make decisions about what is most important to teach. Teachers use the textbook as one lens through which to make teaching decisions. In many districts, even though textbooks are provided, there is not a structured way for deciding how the textbooks are to be used. Do I start at the beginning and teach every page? Do I skip around and only teach what I feel is important? Do I meet with others and decide as a group? The superintendent may feel that textbooks structure what is taught and therefore providing a textbook for teachers and students is important. The actual use of textbooks across a district, however, may be more problematic.

Examining the alignment between textbooks, standards, tests, and instruction is important so we can understand if the textbook is supporting the appropriate teaching and learning spelled out by state standards and state assessments. Most textbooks claim to be aligned to state standards and assessments. The little research that has been done (reported later in this chapter) calls this claim into question.

Other emerging trends will also affect the use of textbooks. As more resources become available on the Internet, the role of the textbook will likely decline. The money spent on textbooks (sometimes $80 to $150 each) may be put to better use for other things (like curriculum development), especially as more resources become available and known on the World Wide Web. The use of textbooks is in a time of transition.

Next, we examine research on textbooks and alignment from the 1980s and 1990s. Some of the first studies on textbook alignment took place in the 1980s and early 1990s and examined the alignment between textbooks and standardized tests. Many studies were part of a large interest by academia during this time on textbooks and their impact on the general nature of education. We will cover these studies first in a section called Textbook to Test Alignment. From the mid-1990s to 2000 very few studies were done on textbook alignment until a group from the American Association for the Advancement of Science (AAAS) launched Project 2061. They developed a set of national science standards and examined math and science textbooks used in secondary schools and their alignment to standards. The work of AAAS is covered in the second section of this chapter. The third section, called Modifying the Use of Textbooks to Improve Alignment, describes two studies in which two districts successfully aligned their textbook material to standardized tests. Presented at the end of the chapter are some ideas for school districts to consider for improving the alignment of their textbooks to standardized tests.

TEXTBOOK TO TEST ALIGNMENT

Freeman et al. (1983) examined the alignment between math textbooks and the standardized tests used during this period. Howson's (1995) work on textbooks in the Third International Mathematics and Science Study (TIMSS) provides an in-depth study of America's use of textbooks compared with other nations.

Textbooks to Test Alignment—Purpose and Approach

Freeman et al. (1983) examined the alignment of content between mathematics textbooks and standardized tests. Freeman and colleagues summarized the standardized test topics using the test specifications of standardized tests. They next delineated coverage of those topics in textbooks. If the textbook covered the tested topic with twenty or more problems in the text, they coded the topic as covered.

Findings

The table in Figure 3.1 summarizes their findings.

Figure 3.1   Percentage of Tested Topics for Fourth-Grade Mathematics Covered in Textbooks

	Textbook			
Test	Addison-Wesley	Holt	Houghton Mifflin	Scott Foresman
MAT (38 topics)	32	50	40	42
Stanford (72 topics)	22	22	21	22
Iowa (66 topics)	26	29	32	26
CTBS-I (53 topics)	32	32	38	36
CTBS-II (61 topics)	28	38	38	34

SOURCE: Adapted from Freeman, Kuhs, Porter, Floden, Schmidt, and Schwille (1983). Used with permission.
NOTE: Percentages are based on topics covered by at least 20 problems in a book.

The tests with the number of topics on the tests are listed in the first column on the left. The textbooks are listed across the top of the chart. The numbers in the boxes represent the percentage of topics on the standardized tests that are covered with at least twenty problems in the book. So, for example, the Addison-Wesley math textbook covers 32% of the thirty-eight topics on the MAT assessment, or approximately one-third of the topics (about twelve topics of thirty-eight). This finding means that one-third of the topics on the standardized test are covered by twenty or more problems in the textbook. Further, twenty-six topics are *not* covered by the requisite twenty problems. If two-thirds of the tested topics lack minimal coverage in the textbook, are students likely to receive instruction aligned with the standardized test?

Further examination of the chart shows that the best alignment is between the Holt math textbook and the MAT test at 50% of the test items covered by 20 or more items in the textbook. We can conclude that topic alignment is a problem on standardized tests when compared with textbooks. The next study provides more information on topic coverage in textbooks.

International Research on Textbooks—Purpose and Approach

Howson (1995), as part of the Third International Mathematics and Science Study (TIMSS), studied one representative textbook used in each of the forty countries participating in the TIMSS research. To conduct the study, Howson used a standardized list of topics for mathematics and science constructed for TIMMS and aligned this list of topics to the topics in the science textbooks. He also studied how the textbooks suggested that the topics be taught in classes. This expands the concept of alignment from just matching content to completing an inventory of how the topics are taught.

Findings

One of the problems is that the textbooks studied fostered a limited range of learning strategies: mainly learning by listening and by practicing a restricted range of techniques in particular 'closed' situations. Learning by reading, by discussion and argument, and in an attempt to acquire the knowledge to solve a problem of one's own choosing are largely ignored. . . . The emphasis is so frequently on problem-solving where the 'problem' is all too often a routine example (Howson, 1995, p. 41).

Howson (1995) also found that

- there is little explanation of why a topic is being studied (p. 41);
- disconnected topics are tenuously linked and motivated (p. 45);
- there are few hints on how to differentiate the text for use with a range of students (pp. 46–47);
- U.S. texts repeat much work from grade to grade (p. 51).

Howson went on to characterize U.S. textbooks:

The problem of the U.S. text is readily identified. . . . Those coding the text for the main TIMSS study found that it contained over three hundred units [a unit is an idea or concept]—each requiring one to three periods of class time! There is material here for three grades' work. Some is review of material covered in previous years, much is new; some reflects all that is novel in the NCTM [National Council of Teachers of Mathematics] Standards (1989), some appears very traditional. Teachers are left, with the aid of a voluminous teachers' guide, to devise a one-year course appropriate for students of very differing abilities and achievements . . . problems of selection of material are great (although advice is to be found in the accompanying guide). . . . The result is that although a study of the Japanese books provides a reasonable idea of what will be taught in their classrooms, just about anything might happen in a U.S. classroom using this particular series of texts. For the U.S. text, although not advertising this fact, is not a *course*, but rather a *resource*. (pp. 28–29)

And, of course, just about anything does happen, especially when there is little guidance. U.S. textbooks, at least the ones in this study, covered more topics than could be reasonably taught in one year. (Other research by AAAS, cited later in this chapter, suggests that this generalization holds across a variety of math and science textbooks.) This demonstrates that using the alignment of textbooks in math and science as a guide for instruction is tenuous. This also illustrates how tenuous the alignment between textbooks and standards is when Howson proclaims that "some reflects all that is novel in the NCTM [National Council of Teachers of Mathematics] Standards (1989), some appears very traditional."

The Dominant Role of Textbooks—Purpose and Approach

Other research completed as part of TIMMS suggests that textbooks play a dominant role in instruction, content, and student achievement. We will further explore the details of how this part of the study was designed in Chapter 7.

Findings

The model in this research study shows . . . the strong role that textbooks played (both directly and in learning mathematics (and science) in eighth grade in the United States). (Schmidt et al., 2001, pp. 282–283)

Figure 3.2 shows that the amount of textbook coverage for a topic in math and science was related to the instructional time teachers spent on the topic and the achievement related to the topic. This shows that textbooks provide teachers with important clues in planning and delivering their instruction. Although the majority of the research reported here is critical of textbooks and their alignment to standards and assessments, it is important to realize that teachers across the world use textbooks as one indicator of what is valuable to cover.

We believe that we found powerful evidence that textbooks exert a strong influence on what teachers teach . . . Textbook coverage is important both for what topics are taught and for the levels of performances and accomplishments expected of students . . . It is perilous to ignore the ways in which they at least partially shape what is taught (Schmidt et al., 2001, p. 357).

If you can't rely on textbooks, what can you rely on?

District Curriculum Guides—Purpose, Approach, and Findings

Floden, Porter, Schmidt, Freeman, and Schwille (1980) found that the content of district curriculum guides did not align well to district adopted texts; but teachers generally followed the textbooks, not the curriculum (textbook to curriculum alignment).

SUMMARY OF FINDINGS FOR STUDIES OF TEXTBOOK TO TEST ALIGNMENT

The studies pointed out two competing trends. The studies quoted in the first section of this chapter showed a lack of alignment between textbooks and standardized tests, curriculum-embedded tests, and instruction. But Schmidt et al. (2001) found a clear alignment between the content of texts, the time devoted to instruction, and the test results, although they were dealing with the TIMSS test results, not state standardized tests. Here's one way to make sense of the competing trends. The work of Schmidt et al. (2001) shows that teachers tend to take direction for their

Figure 3.2   United States: The Relationship of Textbook Coverage to Standards, Instructional Time, and Achievement Gain

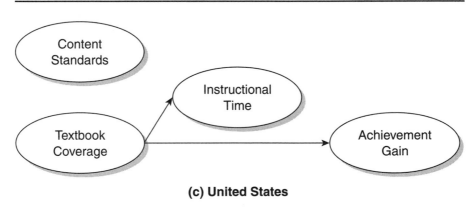

(c) United States

Arrows indicate statistically significant positive relationships; absence indicates no relationship

instruction based on the content of the textbook. Further, when the text is aligned to the assessment (the more the country's text was aligned with the content of the TIMSS test), the more time is spent on tested topics, with the results indicating that the better the alignment between text and test, the better the results.

Howson (1995) suggests that U.S. textbooks cover too many topics, so teachers must choose which ones to teach. Because textbooks are produced nationally, there is little evidence that tested topics are emphasized enough, with so many topics (over three hundred) covered. Teachers looking for guidance on what is most important to cover won't find answers in the textbooks because the textbooks cover "everything" once lightly. Such findings should be a warning to districts: purchasing a textbook as a vehicle to align instruction to standards and state tests will *not* work, at least in the United States.

QUALITY OF TEXTBOOK INSTRUCTION

In this next set of studies we look at AAAS's Project 2061. AAAS evaluated ten to fifteen math and science textbooks for middle and high school. They determined the alignment of the textbooks to a series of benchmarks contained in most state standards (textbook to standards alignment). They also examined the quality of instructional guidance given by the textbook to the teacher (textbook to instruction alignment). Here, alignment is not just the content match but how the content is presented in the text or the quality of instruction.

Science and Math Textbooks and Quality of Instruction—Purpose and Approach

AAAS examined seven qualities:

1. identifying a sense of purpose
2. building on List of Figures ideas
3. engaging students in the subject area
4. developing ideas
5. promoting student thinking
6. assessing student progress
7. enhancing the learning environment

Findings

This information was summarized on a rating scale. Figures 3.3, 3.4, and 3.5 summarize their work.

Figure 3.3   Instructional Ratings of Middle School Mathematics Textbooks

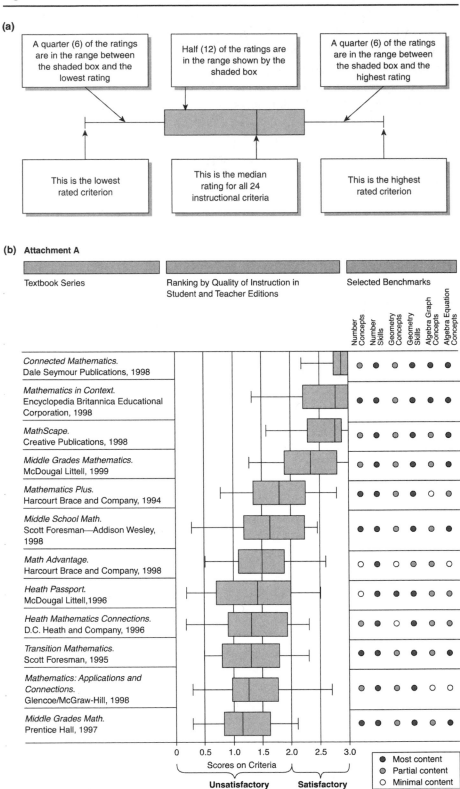

Figure 3.4   Quality Assessment of Middle School Science Texts

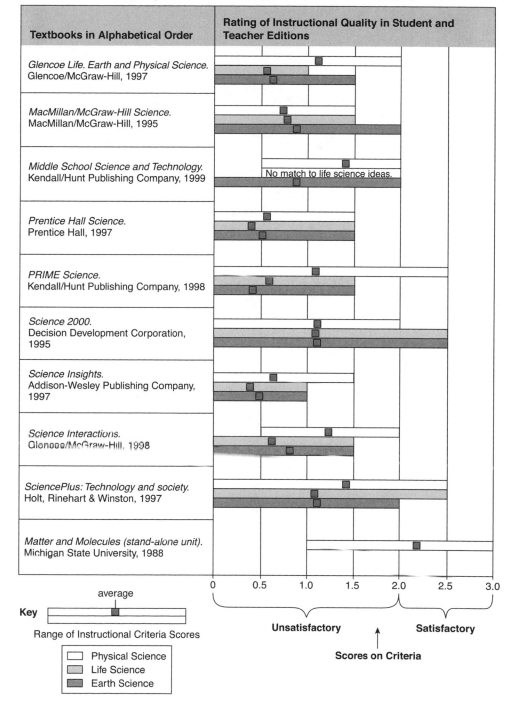

AAAS Project 2061 Middle Grades Science Textbooks Evaluation

Figure 3.5 Project 2061 Instructional Analysis of Biology Textbooks

Average of ratings for four topics — Instructional Categories	*Biology* Miller, Levine Prentice Hall	*Biology: A Community Context* South-Western Educational Publishing	*Biology: Principles and Explorations* Holt, Rinehart and Winston	*Biology: The Dynamics of Life* Glencoe, McGraw-Hill	*Biology: Visualizing Life* Holt, Rinehart and Winston	*BSCS Biology: A Human Approach* Kendall Hunt	*BSCS Biology: An Ecological Approach* Kendall Hunt	*Heath Biology* D.C Health and Company	*Insights in Biology* Kendall Hunt	*Modern Biology* Holt, Rinehart and Winston
I. PROVIDING A SENSE OF PURPOSE										
Conveying unit purpose	Fair	Good	Poor	Poor	Poor	Good	Good	Poor	Fair	Poor
Conveying lesson purpose	Poor	Fair	Poor	Poor	Poor	Satisfactory	Poor	Poor	Satisfactory	Poor
Justifying lesson sequence	Fair	Fair	Fair	Fair	Fair	Fair	Fair	Fair	Fair	Fair
II. TAKING ACCOUNT OF STUDENT IDEAS										
Attending to prerequisite knowledge and skills	Poor	Poor	Poor	Poor	Poor	Poor	Poor	Poor	Poor	Poor
Alerting teacher to commonly held student ideas	Poor	Poor	Poor	Poor	Poor	Poor	Poor	Poor	Poor	Poor
Alerting teacher in identifying own students' ideas	Poor	Poor	Poor	Poor	Poor	Poor	Poor	Poor	Fair	Poor
Addressing commonly held ideas	Poor	Poor	Poor	Poor	Poor	Poor	Poor	Poor	Poor	Poor
III. ENGAGING STUDENTS WITH RELEVANT PHENOMENA										
Providing variety of phenomena	Poor	Poor	Poor	Poor	Poor	Poor	Poor	Poor	Poor	Poor
Providing vivid experiences	Poor	Poor	Poor	Poor	Poor	Poor	Poor	Poor	Poor	Poor
IV. DEVELOPING AND USING SCIENTIFIC IDEAS										
Introducing terms meaningfully	Poor	Poor	Poor	Poor	Poor	Fair	Poor	Poor	Satisfactory	Poor
Representing ideas effectively	Poor	Poor	Poor	Poor	Poor	Poor	Poor	Poor	Poor	Poor
Demonstrating use of knowledge	Poor	Poor	Poor	Poor	Poor	Poor	Poor	Poor	Poor	Poor
Providing practice	Poor	Poor	Poor	Poor	Poor	Poor	Poor	Poor	Poor	Poor
V. PROMOTING STUDENT THINKING ABOUT PHENOMENA, EXPERIENCES, AND KNOWLEDGE										
Encouraging students to explain their ideas	Poor	Poor	Poor	Poor	Poor	Fair	Poor	Poor	Poor	Poor
Guiding students interpretation and reasoning	Poor	Poor	Poor	Poor	Poor	Poor	Poor	Poor	Fair	Poor
Encouraging students to reflect on their own learning	Poor	Poor	Poor	Poor	Poor	Poor	Poor	Poor	Poor	Poor
VI. ASSESSING PROGRESS										
Aligning assessment to goals	Poor	Poor	Poor	Poor	Poor	Poor	Poor	N/A	Poor	Poor
Testing for understanding	Poor	Poor	Poor	Poor	Poor	Poor	Poor	N/A	Poor	Poor
Using assessment to inform instruction	Poor	Poor	Poor	Poor	Poor	Poor	Poor	N/A	Poor	Poor

Project 2061 Instructional Analysis of Biology Textbooks

■ = Excellent (3); ■ = Good (2.5-2.9); □ = Satisfactory (2-2.4); ■ = Fair (1.5-1.9); ■ = Poor (0-1.4)

Figure 3.3 shows the math textbook series in the first column, the scoring of Quality of Instruction in the second column (text to instruction alignment), and coverage or alignment of the text contents to selected benchmarks or standards (text to standards alignment) in the third column (Kulm, Roseman, & Treistman, 1999). Notice that only four of twelve textbooks are rated satisfactory. Only three of the twelve textbooks cover more than three benchmarks well, indicated by a rating of Most Content. This indicates problems in textbooks and their alignment to standards for middle school math texts.

Science texts fared no better when examined with similar criteria.

The first nine textbooks (including books from large publishers) all were rated as unsatisfactory in physical science, life science, and earth science. Six of the ten textbooks received most of their ratings below 1.0 on a 3-point scale, where above 2.0 was considered satisfactory. Only one science text was given a (barely) satisfactory rating for physical science, and this textbook is not widely available. School districts are spending millions of dollars on textbooks that are rated unsatisfactory.

Biology texts were rated similarly.

Figure 3.5 indicates that most biology textbooks are rated below satisfactory on almost all rated categories. Of the nineteen categories rated (see left hand side of chart), only one category—Justifying Lesson Sequence—received a fair rating, while the other eighteen categories were rated as poor for most of the ten textbooks rated here. For example, in the category Aligning Assessments to Goals all books received a poor rating with the exception of one that was not rated.

Reading Texts and Alignment—Purpose and Approach

Reading texts have similarly bad ratings with respect to alignment issues (Manzo, 2007). Goodman, Shannon, Freeman, and Murphy, (1987) analyzed basal readers for elementary schools. They used the word *mismatch* for what we would call misalignment.

Findings

Goodman and his colleagues found:

- a mismatch [misalignment] between basal and standards of expert approaches to reading [text to standards alignment] (p. 66)
- a mismatch [misalignment] between basals and students' prerequisite skills [text to instruction alignment] (p. 69)

- a mismatch [misalignment] between basals' comprehension instruction and students' instructional needs [text to instruction alignment] (p. 82)
- a mismatch [misalignment] between basals' curriculum and the content of the formative assessments included in the basals [text to curriculum-embedded test alignment] (pp. 92, 107, 114, 121)

Most textbook salespeople claim that the texts are aligned to all forty-nine states' standards and assessments (Iowa is the only state that does not have state standards and assessments). But these in-depth analyses of the textbooks indicate a lack of alignment to standards and assessments. This alignment information should provide a cautionary tale for those who think they can rely on textbooks to be the only source of curriculum guidance for a district's teachers.

MODIFYING THE USE OF TEXTBOOKS TO IMPROVE ALIGNMENT

The next two studies show examples of how alignment has been used in the real world of school districts to improve student results within a year's time. These studies reinforce the idea that when districts control their curriculum or materials, assuring alignment with high-stakes tests, results can be both large and positive. An important indicator of quality of instruction highlighted in these studies is the degree of alignment between the curriculum or the curriculum materials and the test.

Systematic Modification of Instructional Materials and Instruction Based on Textbook Alignment—Purpose and Approach

Moss-Mitchell (1998) looked at third-grade mathematics achievement in a large school district (4,000 third graders) in DeKalb County, Georgia, when the district's texts were aligned to the test (text to test alignment). Fifty-five percent of the students were receiving free or reduced lunch, an indication of poverty. The study's purpose was "to examine the implication for educational administrators of effectiveness of the DeKalb County (Georgia) school system's curriculum alignment after one year of implementation" (Moss-Mitchell, 1998, p. 8). The Moss-Mitchell study examined the effects of curriculum alignment when analyzed by students' socioeconomic level, race, gender, and school size.

The district used two approaches to curriculum alignment. Four schools adopted Evans-Newton, Inc., of Scottsdale, Arizona, centering on staff development, monitoring, and managing. The other approach, which was district directed, began with a correlation of the ITBS (Iowa Test of Basic Skills) to the math textbook (textbook to standardized test alignment). Twenty-three percent of the content in the textbook was not covered by the ITBS (Moss-Mitchell, 1998, p. 85), meaning 77% of the content was aligned between the textbook and the test. This reinforces previously reported textbook alignment findings (see Freeman et al., 1983) where the textbook to test alignment was less than 51% in all cases. The district then created or selected additional curricular materials that filled in the gaps between the textbook and the test. Instructional coordinators worked with six schools apiece to help faculty use the additional materials and the curriculum. (This improved the textbook to curriculum alignment, the textbook to instruction alignment, and the textbook to student assignment alignment; it is shown on the alignment matrix for this chapter.)

Findings

At the end of the year, students had improved six NCEs (Normal Curve Equivalent—a scale for averaging student achievement scores) from 49 to 55 on the ITBS standardized test. This was a statistically significant improvement. "There was no statistically significant difference in the effect of curriculum alignment after one year of treatment when analyzed by socioeconomic level, race, gender, or school size" (Moss-Mitchell, 1998, p. 96). This means that traditional predictors of scores, like socioeconomic level or race, did not factor into the improvement in scores. Perhaps ensuring alignment will assist in closing the achievement gap.

Moss-Mitchell's study produced results: the study showed the effects of alignment canceling out more traditional predictors of student achievement such as socioeconomic status, gender, race, or teacher effect. Moss-Mitchell studied the alignment of the textbook with the state mandated standardized test after ensuring alignment with curriculum, student assignments, and instruction.

The Price-Baugh Study: Misalignment May Be Partly Due to the Content of Textbooks—Purpose and Approach

The Price-Baugh study (1997) examined the effects of alignment between text and the state developed test (Texas Assessment of Academic Skills or TAAS) in Houston Independent School district for Grade 7, encompassing 10,233 students in thirty-five middle schools. The textbook content was identified by TAAS descriptors (a similar approach was taken by the Howson study that used TIMSS descriptors). Then, Price-Baugh counted the number of skill-level and application-level word problems for each TAAS descriptor. She then "correlated the amount of practice and explanation in the textbook for 11 target components with the percentage of students correctly answering TAAS problems on those target components" (Price-Baugh, 1997, p. 109). This is an example of a test to textbook alignment. Her findings follow.

Findings

Student achievement was positively correlated with all but one textbook variable. High levels of variance (over 55%) were explained by the "number of available skill-level practice items in the textbook for each target component" (p. 111); the number of pages devoted to practice problems; and the number of application-level problems included in the text. This means, for districts adopting textbooks, that the amount of practice students receive in textbooks or curriculum material on areas that are tested has a significant effect on student achievement. Districts will want to spend time doing their own textbook correlation to state test categories, rather than relying on publisher's correlations because they generally don't include the number of problems in specific areas tested. Like Moss-Mitchell's study, Price-Baugh also confirmed the positive effect of text to standardized test alignment.

The studies discussed in this chapter are charted on the alignment matrix in Figure 3.6.

Figure 3.6   The Alignment Matrix—Textbooks

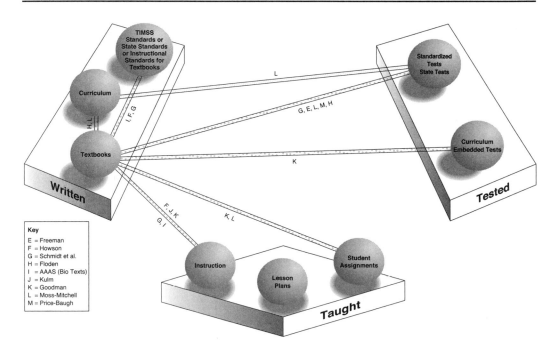

Figure 3.6 shows that research about textbook alignment has focused on instruction, student assignments, curriculum-embedded tests, state tests, state standards, and curriculum, covering all aspects of the written, taught, and tested curriculum.

SUMMARY OF FINDINGS FOR TEXTBOOK ALIGNMENT

All of the authors discussed in this section point out difficulties with relying solely on textbooks to ensure alignment, yet Schmidt et al. (2001) shows that textbooks provide clues that help teachers decide what to emphasize when teaching. Textbooks used in these studies indicate problems with alignment to standards, standardized test specifications, curriculum-embedded tests, curriculum, and instruction. Howson (1995) points out that given the number of topics covered in textbooks (enough to fill three years' worth of instruction), they are best used as a resource rather than a guide for teachers' instructional decisions. This would be a dramatic change in practice, one that would need to be reinforced by staff development initiatives.

WHAT DISTRICTS CAN DO

#3–1

Coverage isn't enough—gather data on student practice opportunities in textbooks.

The Price-Baugh and Floden et al. studies show that coverage is not enough, but student opportunity to practice is important. Districts should obtain the data so they can make a judgment of whether there is enough practice in their materials for instruction that is aligned with high-stakes tests. Here are a couple of ways to gather the information.

Some states don't directly specify what is on their tests. Most states release sample items, such as the document in Figure 3.7 downloaded from the Connecticut State Department of Education Web site (http://www.csde.state.ct.us/public/cedar/assessment/cmt/resources.htm).

Obviously, this is one page of a multipage document, but it is sufficient for an example. On another sheet of paper, place columns that indicate the data you want to retrieve from your textbook. The top section might look like the row shown in Figure 3.8.

Duplicate as many pages as you have pages of items and tape them together. Now proceed through the textbook and make the tallies for the

Figure 3.7   Connecticut Mastery Test—Sample Grade 3 Items

Connecticut Mastery Test – 4th Generation
Mathematics Grade 3 Sample Items – DRAFT

---

1. Place Value - MC

The value of 79 would change by how much if the 7 was replace by a 5?

- ○ 2
- ○ 5
- ◉ 20
- ○ 50

---

2. Pictorial Representations of Numbers - MC

What part of this shape is shaded?

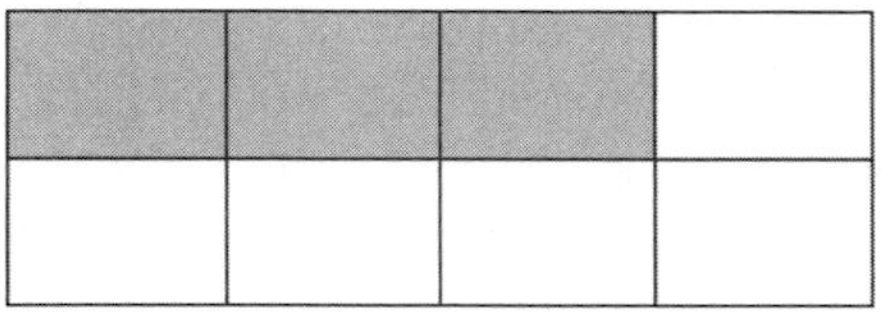

- ○ $\frac{1}{8}$
- ○ $\frac{1}{3}$
- ◉ $\frac{3}{8}$
- ○ $\frac{3}{5}$

---

3. Pictorial Representations of Numbers - OE

Shade in $\frac{5}{6}$ of the figure.

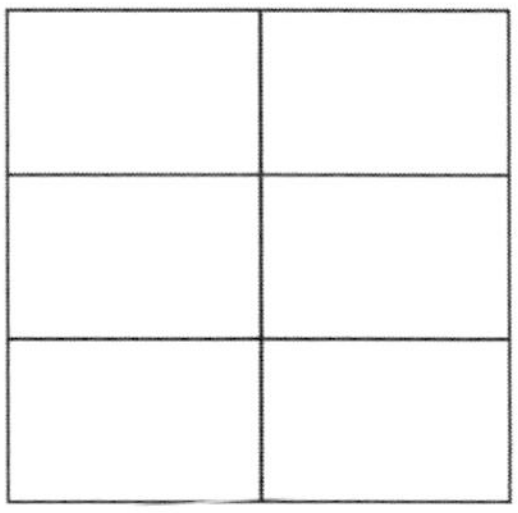

five columns. Many teachers can be involved in this initial activity so all teachers understand how the data was gathered.

Once the initial data is gathered, convene a representative committee for the course or grade level. Ask the committee to make a judgment of whether there is enough practice in the textbook to ensure that all students will be able to do a similar problem on the state test.

For areas not adequately addressed by the textbook, material will have to be found or developed that will provide students with practice for these concepts. Post this material on the district's Web site for ease of distribution.

Finally, adjust the curriculum expectations to ensure that all students have the opportunity for adequate practice on the items. If you don't have a districtwide curriculum, this activity provides a good place to begin. At a minimum, a committee needs to specify the topics and the specific times of the year when they should be covered with a list of locations where practice items can be found (e.g., the text and the district's Web site).

A similar process can be followed if the state gives the test specifications, such as those from Connecticut shown in Figure 3.9 (from http://www.csde.state.ct.uspublic/cedar/assessment/cmt/resources/ctb_presentation/lindabond_ctb_math_presentation.pdf).

Place the topics you are interested in analyzing on the right side. Place the rows shown in Figure 3.8 along the top.

Figure 3.8   Sample Sheet for Determining Amount of Practice for Curriculum Topics

Topic	Textbook or Instructional Material	Number of Pages in the Textbook Generally Addressing This Topic	Number of Problems in the Textbook Addressing This Topic	Number of Practice Items That Look Similar (an Almost Exact Match)

Figure 3.9   Aligning Content Strands From the State Standards to Practice
                  Items in the Textbook

Text Book _____   Grade Level/ Course _____

State Test Specifications CONTENT STRAND	Page Number	Number of Ppractice Problems
Number Sense 1. Place Value 2. Pictorial Representation of Numbers 3. Equivalent Fractions/Decimals/Percents 4. Order/Magnitude/Rounding of Numbers		
Operations 5. Models for Operations 6. Basic Facts 7. Computation With Whole Numbers and Decimals 8. Computation With Fractions 9. Solve Word Problems		
Estimation and Approximation 10. Numerical Estimation Strategies 11. Estimating Solutions to Problems 12. Ratio and Proportion 13. Computation With Percents		
Measurement 14. Time 15. Approximating Measures 16. Customary and Metric Measures		
Spatial Relationships and Geometry 17. Geometric Shapes and Properties 18. Spatial Relationships		
Probability and Statistics 19. Tables, Graphs, and Charts 20. Statistics and Data Analysis 21. Probability		
Patterns 22. Patterns		
Algebra and Functions 23. Algebraic Concepts		
Discrete Mathematics 24. Classification and Logical Reasoning		
Integrated Understandings 25. Mathematical Applications		

Pluses

- This analysis not only matches content but also indexes the amount of practice and the number of textbook pages that address the topic.
- This analysis can be done expeditiously by teaching staff.
- This analysis will point out areas that are not covered with enough material and where the practice is inadequate.

Other Considerations

- Note that this analysis doesn't consider content not covered by the tests. Some content is important but won't be on the test (e.g., listening and speaking in English language arts).
- This will not address all of the standards for the subject area, because state tests don't assess all the standards in all the subject areas.
- This may create the false impression that the district is only interested in alignment to tests. Such data collection and analysis should involve other sources of alignment as well. (Subsequent chapters will have some ideas.)

#3–2

Conduct textbook alignment studies keyed to test results.

Many states offer item analysis reports or cluster analysis reports that show how students did on various items or sections of the state assessment. Conduct similar analyses to the one above, but instead of using all the clusters, use only those where students did very well and those where they did poorly. Gather the data for each grade level or course that leads up to the test. Then compare the number of textbook pages and the amount of practice for students on the high versus low items. Any patterns in the data? Generally you may find that clusters where students did well, there was adequate practice, and those where students did poorly, there was inadequate practice. If this isn't the case, can you figure out why? Did kids score well but not have much practice because practice was provided at previous grade levels? Did kids score poorly but get a lot of practice? Maybe they should have been introduced to the topic at a previous grade level so the instructional sequence for that cluster wouldn't be as demanding, and students could actually practice to mastery.

Similar data analysis could take place with curriculum-embedded tests or quarterly assessments, provided that the quarterly assessments have been developed according to written test specifications. Just obtaining a copy of the state test (or a sample state test) is no guarantee that you know the test specifications. If only the sample state test is available, you may have to infer the test specifications from the sample test itself. Your inferences may or may not be correct.

Pluses

- Test results are being used to feed data back into your system to improve it.
- Students will be better prepared for next year's test because areas of weakness have been directly addressed and the curriculum subsequently changed for the following year.

Other Considerations

- Some states don't publish sample items or cluster specifications. (Pressure should be brought to these states so that they share the test specifications.) Districts can still complete the analysis using their own testing products (quarterly assessments or district developed curriculum-embedded tests.)

#3–3

Preview textbook purchases by analyzing practice opportunities for areas of weakness.

Before making textbook decisions, conduct an analysis of textbook to state test match. If a complete analysis is too time consuming, choose areas the district has shown weakness in on previous state tests. Examine the amount of practice students actually get on areas tested by the state test.

Pluses

- Data can be used to make a judgment of whether there is adequate practice on areas tested by the state.
- The district will know before purchasing the texts whether deficiencies in coverage exist and then can rectify the situation by supplementing material and instructional strategies on a districtwide basis.

Other Considerations

- Data is only gathered on textbook to test alignment. An important topic may be covered in the textbook, but not covered on the test, and would be missed in this analysis.

#3–4

Survey teachers to determine the time spent on textbook topics before establishing district guidelines of time to be spent on topics.

Combining this data collection activity with one of the previous activities that gathers data on the alignment of textbooks to tests will assist a district in determining guidelines for the amount of time to be spent on curriculum topics. Figure 3.10 shows a sheet that might be given to all sixth-grade teachers in the district. The sheet requests identifying information, and then requests that teachers specify the number of days and the pages not covered in the textbook.

Once this data has been collected and collated, a district mathematics committee may want to examine it for the high and low number of days spent on each chapter, by teacher and by school, to determine patterns. Teachers may allocate very different amounts of time to coverage. The committee may want to check with teachers who vary greatly from others to determine their rationale for their decisions about time for coverage. The committee may then determine if there is an appropriate amount of time to spend on each unit, based on the data from the survey. Such time allocations can be very useful to beginning teachers as they make decisions about depth of coverage for each unit. Alternatively, a survey could be developed that would gather information on how much time was spent with each activity for each unit. Results could point to topics where teachers may need staff development to improve their skills and lessen the amount of time it takes to cover a topic.

Pluses

- Providing teachers with a district-developed timeline for coverage of textbook units sets a standard that will assist beginning teachers in planning coverage during the year.

- Anomalies in the data may indicate where potential difficulties lie as well as the need for further staff development in a particular area.

Other Considerations

- Providing district guidance for time on units may be perceived as limiting the flexibility teachers need to determine appropriate times needed for coverage.

Figure 3.10 Aligning Textbook Topics to Teachers' Use of Instructional Time

School _____

Teacher _____ Date _____

Houghton-Mifflin Grade 6 Mathematics Units	Number of Days	Pages Not Covered
1: Operations With Whole Numbers and Decimals		
2: Data Analysis and Statistics		
3: Fractions and Number Theory		
4: Operations With Fractions		
5: Integers and Rational Numbers		
6: Expressions and Equations		
7: Ratio, Proportion, and Percent		
8: Application of Percent		
9: Geometry of Plane Figures		
10: Geometry and Measurement		
11: Statistics and Probability		
12: Coordinate Graphing, Equations, and Integers		
Other:		
Total (Total should add up to at least 170 days.)		

Alignment of Standards and Standardized Tests

In this chapter, we will examine the research surrounding alignment of standards and standardized, or high-stakes, tests to other areas of the alignment matrix. Standards generally define what students should know and be able to do. Standards describe what student should learn. Standardized (or state) tests are there to assess how well students perform on the standards. We know that it is not possible to assess all standards, so tests are designed to sample the most important standards. For example, language arts standards generally have categories of reading, writing, speaking, and listening. Yet most state tests only assess reading and writing, even though many states have standards for speaking and listening as well.

The relationship between standards and standardized tests is the alignment area that has been most heavily studied. As states developed their standards and assessments, they needed ways to ensure that the state assessments were aligned to the state standards. Many of the studies reported here show disparities (nonalignment) between state standards and state assessments.

What are some of the other relationships between standards and standardized assessments and the other components of the alignment matrix? The studies covered in this chapter are placed on the alignment matrix in Figure 4.1.

Figure 4.1   The Alignment Matrix—State Assessments

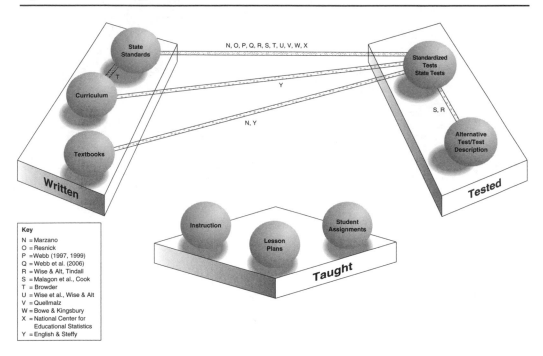

Key
N = Marzano
O = Resnick
P = Webb (1997, 1999)
Q = Webb et al. (2006)
R = Wise & Alt, Tindall
S = Malagon et al., Cook
T = Browder
U = Wise et al., Wise & Alt
V = Quellmalz
W = Bowe & Kingsbury
X = National Center for
      Educational Statistics
Y = English & Steffy

The alignment matrix for standardized tests shows that the majority of work has been completed in aligning state tests and state standards. This is understandable because there are enormous policy implications for the forty-nine states that have state standards and tests. Little research has been done aligning state tests to district assessments, student assignments, teacher lesson plans, or instruction.

MARZANO'S STANDARDS COMPILATION AND THE WEB SITE FOR ACHIEVE, INC.—PURPOSE AND APPROACH

At the very beginning of the standards movement, Kendall and Marzano (1997a) suggested that districts develop their own standards. Then Marzano, while at Midwestern Regional Educational Laboratory (MCREL), saw the need to compile the standards from states and national professional associations into one document. He then synthesized all of the standards for each subject area into one set of standards for the subject area, published in book and CD-ROM format as *Content Knowledge: A Compendium of Standards and Benchmarks for K–12 Education* (Kendall & Marzano, 1997b). The *Content Knowledge* volume is most useful to those who want to create their own district standards using this document as a template, and it provides one synthesis of important ideas that are encompassed in many of the states' standards documents.

Marzano then used these standards as benchmarks for comparing any state's or national professional association's standards to each other. He created a Web site where queries for any state can be made to compare (align) one set of standards to another. Commercial applications allow test makers or textbook companies to align their tests and materials with all state standards at once. The Achieve, Inc. Web site is at www.achieve.org.

Achieve has four criteria (Resnick, Rothman, Slattery, & Vranek, 2003) for alignment of assessments or textbooks to standards:

- **Content.** Does the test measure what the state standards indicate that all students should know and be able to do at a particular grade level? If not, is it because the standards are too vague to make a determination, or is it because test items measure only part of what the standards ask for?
- **Performance.** Are students asked to demonstrate the skills the standards expect? For example, if the standards say that students will analyze the characteristics of various literary forms, does the test ask them to evaluate different literary forms, or does it merely ask students to identify one type of literature?
- **Level of Difficulty.** Are test items easy, medium, or hard, and is the range of difficulty appropriately distributed across all the items? What makes them difficult—the content they are assessing or another factor, such as the language of the question? Overall, is each assessment appropriately rigorous for students who have been taught to the state standards?
- **Balance and Range.** Does the test as a whole gauge the depth and breadth of the standards and objectives outlined in state standards documents? If not, are the standards that are assessed the most important for the grade level? Overall, do the assessments for elementary, middle, and high school focus on the most important content that all students should know?

Findings

The meaning of alignment has been further differentiated so that a match is not just a match of one set of content to another but also to other characteristics, such as balance and range or level of difficulty. Alignment is becoming more precise yet more difficult. Currently, Achieve provides alignment services for states and districts, particularly in alignment of assessments to state standards with other services, such as standards benchmarking and augmentation analysis, where off-the-shelf tests are compared with a state's standards (Council of Chief State School Officers, 2003).

The alignment matrix at the beginning of this chapter shows that Marzano's products look at the alignment between state standards, state tests, and textbooks. Webb's studies, which we will examine next, look at the relationship between state standards and standardized tests.

THE WEBB STUDIES: ALIGNING STATE STANDARDS, ASSESSMENTS, AND POLICIES—PURPOSE AND APPROACH

Webb (1997) found ways to confirm the alignment between state standards and state assessments. Webb examined three approaches toward alignment. The first, Sequential Development, means developing documents in sequence so the first document (e.g., state standards) is aligned and used as a reference for the second document (e.g., curriculum frameworks or assessments). The second approach, Expert Review, uses experts to review the alignment between standards and assessments. The third approach (described in Chapter 7 with TIMSS, in Porter's work, and in this chapter's discussion of Marzano's work) creates a common description of curriculum, then analyzes the alignment between the common descriptions and other parts of the educational system, such as standards, assessments, instruction, and instructional plans. None of these approaches has specific criteria for judging alignment; in many cases it is a case of alignment or nonalignment based strictly on the content of the standards and the content of the assessment. Webb's contribution is his development of five major criteria for alignment of expectations (standards) and assessments in math and science education. Additionally, Webb put into perspective the complete range of alignment possibilities to include such ideas as policy elements and the use of technology, materials, and tools. Webb applied his ideas to examining the alignment between expectations (standards) and assessments for four states, using some of the criteria for alignment he proposed.

Webb (1997) begins by discussing the concept of alignment:

> Two or more system components are aligned if they are in agreement or match each other. . . . Alignment is being used to characterize the agreement or match among a set of documents or multiple components of a state or district system. (p. 3)

Then Webb defines alignment. *"Alignment* is the degree to which expectations and assessments are in agreement and serve in conjunction with one another to guide the system towards students learning what they are expected to know and do" (p. 4).

Note that Webb is focusing here on alignment between assessments (state tests) and expectations (state standards).

Webb then developed criteria for judging alignment. This continues the expansion of the concept of alignment. The first area of alignment in Webb's study is concerned with content focus, that is, how closely the expectations (standards) and the assessments (state tests) share the following attributes.

The first attribute is categorical congruence, that is, the same categories of content appear both in the standards and in the test. For example, if "problem solving" appeared as a major heading in the standards, we would look for "problem solving" to be a major heading in the test specifications. This is consistent with previous ways of determining alignment.

The second attribute, depth of knowledge, involves the cognitive complexity of the information (Figure 4.2) and the transfer of this knowledge to new situations. For example, the standards might state that students should design, conduct, and interpret a statistical experiment. The assessment would have the same depth of knowledge if students were provided with the opportunity to design, conduct, and interpret a statistical experiment. If students only had the opportunity to design the experiment, but not to conduct or interpret it, the depth of knowledge on the assessment would be less and the alignment weak.

The third attribute, range of knowledge correspondence, indicates whether standards and assessments "cover a comparable span of topics and ideas within categories" (Webb, 1997). For example, if the standards state that students should be able to read four different types of maps and the assessment tests students' ability to read four different types of maps, the alignment would be perfect. Because of the short amount of time devoted to testing, generally not all standards will be completely assessed. The assessment may only test the students' knowledge of one type of map.

The fourth and last attribute is balance of representation. All of the standards need to be represented in the assessments. When balance of representation is lacking, students could be judged with the test—as meeting the expectations or standards—even though they have not been tested on all the standards.

The second level in Webb's alignment analysis consisted of a rating of depth of knowledge of the objectives. This was a way to see if the standards required the same depth of knowledge as is required in the specifications for the state assessments.

Figure 4.2   Depth of Knowledge Categories

1. Recall Recall of a fact, information, or procedure.
2. Skill/Concept Use of information, conceptual knowledge, procedures, two or more steps, etc.
3. Strategic Thinking Requires reasoning, developing a plan or sequence of steps; has some complexity; more than one possible answer; generally takes less than 10 minutes to do.
4. Extended Thinking Requires an investigation; time to think and process multiple conditions of the problem or task; and more than 10 minutes to do non-routine manipulations.

Webb trained coders from the four states studied to validly and reliably rate the alignment between the state standards (expectations) and the state assessments.

Findings

A summary of Webb's alignment results is shown in Figure 4.3. The columns show:

- the state
- the content area
- the grade where students were assessed
- the number of state standards and the number of state objectives
- the number of items in the state assessment
- the percent of standards with acceptable alignment

In the depth-of-knowledge category, no item aligned 100%, showing that the state tests studied do not assess for the same depth of knowledge as proposed by the state standards.

Most of the alignments cover the areas of skill/concept and strategic thinking. Few objectives dealt only with recall and extended thinking. Extended thinking involved a problem that might take at least ten minutes to do; even so, there were quite a number of extended thinking items on the assessments.

The alignment area with the fewest alignments is range of knowledge correspondence. Being insufficient in the range of knowledge

Figure 4.3   Summary of Alignment Analysis for State Standards and State Tests

State	Content Area	Grade	Standard N	Obj N	Depth of Knowledge Level of Objectives				Item[b] N	Students With Percent Acceptable Alignment by Criteria[a]			
					Recall %	Skill/ Concept %	Strategic Thinking %	Extended Thinking %		Cat. Concurr %	Depth %	Range %	Balance %
A	Science	3	6	61	16	61	23	0	44	67	83	33	100
		8	6	97	9	56	33	2	70	67	17	33	100
	Mathematics	3	6	94	15	45	26	13	50	67	50	0	100
		6	6	101	10	49	27	14	61	100	100	0	83
B	Mathematics	4	7	61	2	56	34	8	86	100	57	57	86
		8	7	43	0	42	42	16	86	100	71	86	71
		10	4	20	0	35	65	0	70	100	0	100	100
C	Science	4	5	60	8	72	20	0	14	und[c]	und	und	und
		8	5	86	7	77	16	0	14	und	und	und	und
	Mathematics	4	6	107	6	61	31	3	74	100	100	33	83
		8	6	105	11	42	32	12	68	83	83	0	83
D	Science	3	8	86	14	57	20	9	50	38	25	0	100
		7	8	93	11	64	22	3	49	62	50	25	100
		10	8	72	1	56	33	10	46	62	12	12	100
	Mathematics	4	10	56	0	21	41	38	54	90	40	80	90
		8	10	63	0	17	38	44	51	50	40	30	80

SOURCE: From *Determining alignment of expectations and assessments in mathematics and science education*, by N. L. Webb (1997, January). NISE Brief, 1. Madison: Wisconsin Center for Education Research, National Institute for Science Education, University of Wisconsin. Reprinted with permission.

NOTE: a. Categorical Concurrence
   Depth of Knowledge Consistency
   Range of Knowledge Correspondence
   Balance of Representation

   b. Total number of assessment items

   c. und—undetermined because too few and only sample items were included in the analysis

correspondence means "Important forms or specific cases of major concepts or ideas given in the expected performance are excluded from or ignored on assessments or their specifications" (Webb, 1997). This observation may be partially explained by comparing the number of objectives on the test with the number of items. In most cases there are more objectives than there are items.

Figure 4.3 also indicates that different states and different tests within the same states have different alignment characteristics. For example, in State C's science test at Grade 4 and 8, there were insufficient items to determine categorical congruence, depth, range, or balance. On the other hand, State B's mathematics test for Grade 8 showed the highest overall alignment.

Teachers and administrators need to understand how well their state tests are aligned to their state standards. If the alignment is high, then coverage of the standards is likely to produce high scores on the tests. On the other hand, if the alignment is low or nonexistent between the state standards and the assessments, then the test specifications need to be closely examined and the alignment with the district curriculum determined.

More general findings about alignment of state standards to assessments follow:

> The analyses indicated that the standards of the four states varied in what content students were expected to know, the level of specificity at which expectations were expressed, and organization . . . . Alignment between assessments and standards varied across grade levels, content areas, and states without any discernable pattern. Assessments and standards of three of the four states satisfied the categorical congruence criterion. This criterion, the most common conception of alignment, required the assessment and standards to include the same content topics. Alignment was found to be the weakest on the depth of knowledge consistency and range of knowledge correspondence criteria. Generally, assessment items required a lower level of knowledge and did not span the full spectrum of knowledge as expressed in the standards. However, for the knowledge and skills identified in the standards and addressed by the assessments, generally the assessment items were evenly distributed. (Webb, 1997, p. vii)

Webb shows that standards and assessments can be aligned using valid and reliable criteria and shows how the process was used in conducting an analysis of alignment on standards and assessments from four states.

Districts could also use such a process as they seek to align their curriculum-embedded assessments to state standards or the significant tasks in their curriculum to state standards and assessments (Webb, 1999).

WEBB'S WAT WEB SITE—PURPOSE AND APPROACH

Webb, Alt, Ely, Cormier, and Vesperman (2006) now have developed a Web-based tool and training system that makes Webb's processes for aligning state standards and assessments automated and accessible to anyone. With access to the state assessments, anyone can create their own valid and reliable studies of alignment between state standards and state assessments. The tool, called the Web Alignment Tool or WAT, is available at the Web site http://www.wcer.wisc.edu/WAT/.

Findings

The Webb process has also been used to align alternative assessments appropriate for special education students to state standards (Tindall, 2006; Wise & Alt, 2006). Assessments included performance assessments and portfolio assessments for two unnamed states' special education students. The Web site allows creation of an alignment study between the assessments and the standards. As the paper describes specific alignment procedures, these procedures could be replicated for districts interested in how their assessment system aligns to state standards by using the WAT. The Web site can also align English Language Proficiency assessments used with English Language Learners to state standards (Cook, 2006; Malagon, Rosenberg, & Winter, 2006). Webb's work is a great example of how a decade of research results became a useful tool for state departments of education and others to validly and reliably conduct alignment studies.

THE BROWDER STUDY: ALIGNMENT IN SPECIAL EDUCATION—PURPOSE AND APPROACH

The next study, Browder et al. (2004), is another example of alignment of instruction in special education. The 1997 amendments to the Individuals with Disabilities Education Act (IDEA) required states to provide access to the general curriculum and alternate assessments for student with disabilities who were unable to participate in statewide assessment. Previous alternative assessments had been aligned to the functional curriculum that guided special education students' progress. Requiring alternative assessments to align with the subject area state standards provided a paradigm shift. No longer was alignment to the functional curriculum enough. Now, the alternative assessments had to align with the state standards for all students. The purpose of the study by Browder et al. (2004) was to examine the alignment of the content on alternate assessments to academic standards and functional life domains. Three types of assessment questions were categorized: Were the assessments still aligned with the older functional curriculum? Or were the assessments aligned with the subject area state standards? Or was there a combination of assessments that focused both on the functional curriculum and the state standards? The authors hypothesized that "curriculum transformation would be evident if these examples were closely aligned (to the subject-based state standards)" (Browder et al., 2004, p. 213).

"Data were collected from content experts and stakeholders who reviewed the examples of extended state standards provided in states' alternate assessment materials" (p. 213). The content experts followed Crocker and Algina's (1986) process for content validation:

1. Define the performance domains of interest.

2. Select a panel of qualified experts.

3. Provide a structured framework for the process of matching items to the performance domains.

4. Collect and analyze the responses.

The alternative assessments from thirty-one states were collected along with the standards and performance indicators for language arts and math.

Findings

The experts found that some of the alternative assessments were aligned to subject area performance indicators and standards. Eighty-six percent of the math experts and 70% of the language arts experts indicated that some states' lists of performance indicators were clearly linked to the subject area standards. (Colorado provided a superior example.) Conversely, 78% of the language arts experts agreed that some of the performance indicators clearly were *not* aligned to language arts standards. There appeared to be general agreement on whether the standards aligned well or did not align well.

Sixty percent of the experts in severe disabilities stated that the states overall did not do a good job of aligning the general curriculum with their performance indicators, although one state, Connecticut, was cited as an example of properly assessing the general curriculum. Eleven of the thirty-one states incorporated both the academic standards and the functional skills curriculum in their performance assessments, and the experts noted that the blending of functional and academic curriculum provided some of the strongest examples of alignment between standards and alternative assessments. The authors concluded with some policy recommendations for alternative assessment practices.

This study demonstrates that the alignment process may be linked to the problem of content validation, a part of modern test theory. Although the specifics of the alignment process were not clear in the article, it may be that content validation work needs to be expanded into the field of aligning curriculum, standards, and assessments.

VERTICAL ALIGNMENT—PURPOSE AND APPROACH

Vertical alignment examines whether standards and tests at one grade level are built upon the standards and tests at the previous grade levels. The diagram in Figure 4.4 suggests how this might look on the alignment matrix with a comparison of how Grade 4 standards and assessments are aligned with Grade 5 standards and assessments.

The other areas of the alignment matrix are not covered in these investigations.

Two papers deal with vertical alignment: Wise and Alt (2006) and Wise, Zhang, Winter, Taylor, & Becke (2006). Four questions guided the first study:

- What level of concurrence is there between objectives for the two grades?
- To what extent do comparable objectives increase in depth from one grade to the next?
- To what extent does the range of content increase from one grade to the next?
- How does the balance of representation change from one grade to the next?

The results were used to suggest improvements in the alignment of one grade level's standards to the next grade level's standards.

Figure 4.4 Vertical Alignment Between Grade Levels

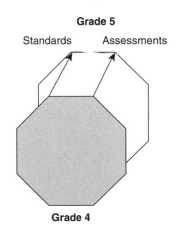

Grade 5

Standards   Assessments

Grade 4

Findings

The results followed Webb's formulation using four alignment categories:

Categorical Concurrence. Results for each standard are summarized by a simple listing of the objectives common to, or at least partially covered in, both grades and the objectives unique to the lower or higher grades. The ratio of the number of common standards to the total number of standards serves as an overall indicator of alignment.

Depth of Knowledge. Increases in depth of knowledge can be assessed by computing the proportion of objectives at one grade that are judged to be covered in greater depth by corresponding objectives at the next higher grade. Note that simple comparisons of the depth of knowledge ratings from a Webb assessment of test alignment may be misleading. A skill which involves deduction or novel application at one grade can become much more routine at a higher grade. In this case, the same skill would be judged to be lower depth at the higher grade, running counter to expectations that depth should increase over grades.

Range of Knowledge. Increases in range of knowledge can be assessed by computing the proportion of objectives at one grade that are judged to be covered more broadly by corresponding objectives at the next higher grade and also the proportion of objectives at the higher grade that are new.

Balance of Representation. Grade-to-grade changes in the balance of representation can be assessed by counting the number of objectives in each of the broad area of standards for each grade. Alternatively, representation could be assessed in terms of the number of test questions targeted for each of the broad standards (Wise & Alt, 2006, pp. 65–66).

This process was field-tested using Delaware's new grade level expectations (GLEs) in English language arts and mathematics for Grades 3 and 10 (Wise et al., 2006). This looked at the vertical alignment of the GLEs. For example, did Grade 3 GLEs provide a base on which Grade 4 GLEs were built? While inter-rater reliability was marginal, the process did expose where the GLEs could be improved.

QUELLMALZ, KREIKEMEIER, HAYDEL DEBARGER, AND HAERTEL USES AN ALIGNMENT PROCESS TO REFINE MEANING OF A STANDARD ON SCIENCE INQUIRY AND COMPARE THE ALIGNMENT OF SCIENCE INQUIRY TO THREE LARGE-SCALE ASSESSMENTS—PURPOSE AND APPROACH

Quellmalz et al. (2006) were first interested in examining the meaning of science inquiry before examining the alignment of science inquiry standards to three tests: the National Assessment of Educational Progress (NAEP), the TIMSS test, and the New Standards Science Reference Exam (NSSRE)—an exam many states have considered using for their science tests.

These researchers began by examining the science inquiry standards of the National Science Education Standards (NSES) put forth by the National Research Council in order to understand the components and design an alignment protocol. After examining the NSES standards about inquiry (science inquiry is one of seven major content standards in science), they found that "descriptions of the NSES inquiry skills were so global or overlapping that clear classification was problematic" (p. 2). Test items were tentatively classified by a panel of national science assessment experts and then given to students who were asked to think about the items aloud. These think alouds and additional interviews with the students were used to confirm the expert judgments and also expand on unclear areas of the standards. Based on these data, the meanings of the standards were clarified. Figure 4.5 shows the initial standards on the left with the clarified standards on the right.

The clarified standards on the right were then used to determine the alignment of the clarified standards with the three tests. A complete listing of the meaning of science inquiry is outlined in Figure 4.6.

Figure 4.5   NSES Inquiry Standards Segmented Into Component Codes and Descriptions

5-8 NSES Inquiry Ability	Component Code Descriptions
5-8.1 Identify questions that can be answered through scientific investigations:	5-8.1.1 Clarify or narrow the focus of questions that guide investigations
Students should develop the ability to refine and refocus broad and ill-defined questions. An important aspect of the ability consists of students' ability to clarify questions and inquiries and direct them toward objects and phenomena that can be described, explained, or predicted by scientific investigations. Students should develop the ability to identify the scientific ideas, concepts, and quantitative relationships that guide investigations.	5-8.1.2 Identify scientific ideas, concepts and quantitative relationships that guide investigations
	5-8.1.3 Identify questions and inquiries that are directed toward observations and measures of objects and natural phenomena

Figure 4.5 NSES Inquiry Standards Segmented Into
Component Codes and Descriptions *(continued)*

5-8 NSES Inquiry Ability	Component Code Descriptions
5-8.2 Design and conduct a scientific investigation: Students should develop general abilities such as systematic observations and accurate measurements, and identifying and controlling variables. They should also develop the ability to clarify ideas that influence and guide the inquiry and to understand how those ideas compare with current scientific knowledge. Students can learn to formulate questions, design investigations, execute investigations, (see InqC) interpret data, use data to generate explanations, propose alternative explanations, and critique explanations and procedures.	5-8.2.1 Identify and control appropriate variables
	5-8.2.2 Describe how to collect systematic observation and/or detect inaccuracies
	5-8.2.3 Describe how to collect accurate measurements and/or detect errors in measurement
	5-8.2.4 Describe how to interpret/ analyze data
5-8.3. Use appropriate tools and techniques to gather, analyze, and interpret data: The use of tools and techniques, including mathematics and computers, will be guided by the question asked and the investigations students design. The use of computers for the collection, summary, and display of evidence is part of this standard. Students should be able to access, gather, store, retrieve, and organize data using hardware and software designed for these purposes.	5-8.3.1 Describe / use tools and techniques to gather data
	5-8.3.2 Describe / use tools and techniques to organize data

Figure 4.6 NSES Science Inquiry Component Codes

Science Inquiry Standards and Target Codes	
Standard 5-8.1: Ask questions 5-8.1.1 Clarify or narrow the focus of questions that guide investigations 5-8.1.2I dentify scientific ideas, concepts and quantitative relationships that guide investigations 5-8.1.3 Identify questions and inquiries that are directed toward observations and measures of objects and natural phenomena	**Standard 5-8.2: Design and conduct experiments** 5-8.2.1 Identify and control appropriate variables 5-8.2.2 Describe how to collect systematic observation and/or detect inaccuracies 5-8.2.3 Describe how to collect accurate measurements and/or detect errors in measurement 5-8.2.4 Describe how to interpret/analyze data
Standard 5-8.3: Use tools and techniques 5-8.3.1 Describe/use tools and techniques to gather data 5-8.3.2 Describe/use tools and techniques to organize data	**Standard 5-8.4: Use evidence to explain** 5-8.4.1 Describe observations made during experiment 5-8.4.2 Use evidence, logical argument, and subject matter knowledge to explain 5-8.4.3 Use evidence, logical argument, and subject matter knowledge to predict 5-8.4.4 Use evidence, logical argument, and subject matter knowledge to create models

Standard 5-8.5: Think critically and logically	Standard 5-8.6: Alternative explanations
5-8.5.1 Decide what evidence to use	5-8.6.1 Identify different ideas
5-8.5.2 Decide how to account for anomalous data	5-8.6.2 Consider alternative explanations
5-8.5.3 Review and summarize data to form a logical argument	
5-8.5.4 Describe or explain possible cause-effect relationships between two or more variables	
Standard 5-8.7: Communication	**Standard 5-8.8: Use mathematics**
5-8.7.1 Describe observations to new audience	5-8.8.1 Use mathematics to structure questions and explanations
5-8.7.2 Summarize results to new audience	5-8.8.2 Use mathematics to gather, organize, and present data
	5-8.8.3 Use mathematics to answer questions

This clarified list of standards was then aligned by the assessment experts to the three tests.

The alignment process followed similar procedures to Webb (1997) to establish categorical concurrence, that is, the categories on the test are similar to the categories in the standards. National science assessment experts used the standards in Figure 4.6 to code each item on each test. Figure 4.7 highlights what they found.

Inquiry items made up a significant percentage of the testing, with almost all performance tasks being inquiry related.

Figure 4.7   Alignment of NAEP, TIMSS, and NSSRE Items in Different Item Formats With Inquiry Standards

	ALL test items (N=677)	Multiple-choice (N=339)	Constructed-response (N=261)	All items w/in a performance task (N=77)
Non-Inquiry	61.7% (418)	64.6% (270)	33.5% (140)	1.9% (8)
Inquiry	38.3% (259)	26.6% (69)	46.7% (121)	89.6% (69)

Figure 4.8 Classification of Science Items as Non-Inquiry or Inquiry Items From NAEP 1996 and 2000

	NAEP 1996 (N=133)	NAEP 2000 (N=197)
Non-Inquiry	45.1% (60)	60.4% (119)
Inquiry	54.9% (73)	39.6% (78)

Two different test administrations of the NAEP were coded, one for 1996 and one for 2000 (Figure 4.8). Surprisingly, there was a significant decline in the percentage of items that tested inquiry on the 2000 test. (This is surprising because when two versions of a test are given, there is an assumption that the tests cover the same content. For science inquiry, this didn't happen with the two versions of the NAEP). The same finding was also true for the three versions of the TIMSS tests examined.

Findings

The next chart (Figure 4.9) summarizes the alignment of all three tests to the modified standards.

The chart shows that different inquiry standards are addressed by different assessments.

Figure 4.9 Classification of NAEP, TIMSS, and NSSRE Inquiry Items Into Inquiry Ability or Component

NSES Inquiry Ability	All NAEP ($N = 97$)	All TIMSS ($N = 112$)	NSSRE ($N = 50$)
Inquiry 5-8.1 Identify questions that can be answered through scientific investigations			
Inquiry 5-8.1.1 Clarify or narrow the focus of questions that guide investigations			
Inquiry 5-8.1.2 Identify scientific ideas, concepts, and quantitative relationships that guide investigations			
Inquiry 5-8.1.3 Identify questions and inquiries that are directed toward observations and measures of objects and natural phenomena	0%	.90% (1)	0%
Inquiry 5-8.2 Design and conduct a scientific investigation	4.1% (4)	.90% (1)	0%
Inquiry 5-8.2.1 Identify and control appropriate variables	3.1% (3)	4.5% (5)	0%
Inquiry 5-8.2.2 Describe how to collect systematic observation and/or detect inaccuracies	2.1% (2)	1.8% (2)	0%
Inquiry 5-8.2.3 Describe how to collect accurate measurements and/or detect errors in measurement	0%	.90% (1)	0%
Inquiry 5-8.2.4 Describe how to interpret/analyze data			

Inquiry 5-8.3 Use appropriate tools and techniques to gather, analyze, and interpret data	0%	.09% (1)	0%
Inquiry 5-8.3.1 Describe/use tools and techniques to gather data	4.1% (4)	2.7% (3)	10.0% (5)
Inquiry 5-8.3.2 Describe/use tools and techniques to organize data	1.0% (1)	.90% (1)	0%
Inquiry 5-8.4 Develop descriptions, explanations, predictions, and models using evidence	2.1% (2)	0%	0%
Inquiry 5-8.4.1 Describe observations made during experiment	3.1% (3)	.90% (1)	0%
Inquiry 5-8.4.2 Use evidence, logical argument, and subject matter knowledge to explain	16.5% (16)	16.1% (18)	20.0% (10)
Inquiry 5-8.4.3 Use evidence, logical argument, and subject matter knowledge to predict	3.1% (3)	9.8% 11)	18.0% (9)
Inquiry 5-8.4.4 Use evidence, logical argument, and subject matter knowledge to create models	1.0% (1)	.90% (1)	2.0% (1)
Inquiry 5-8.5 Think critically and logically to make the relationships between evidence and explanations			
Inquiry 5-8.5.1 Decide what evidence to use	0%	0%	4.0% (2)
Inquiry 5-8.5.2 Decide how to account for anomalous data			
Inquiry 5-8.5.3 Review and summarize data to form a logical argument	0%	0%	2.0% (1)
Inquiry 5-8.5.4 Describe or explain possible cause-effect relationships between two or more variables	0%	.90% (1)	2.0% (1)
Inquiry 5-8.6 Recognize and analyze alternative explanations and predictions			
Inquiry 5-8.6.1 Identify different ideas			
Inquiry 5-8.6.2 Consider alternative explanations	1.0% (1)	0%	0%
Inquiry 5-8.7 Communicate scientific procedures and explanations			
Inquiry 5-8.7.1 Describe observations to new audience			
Inquiry 5-8.7.2 Summarize results to new audience			
Inquiry 5-8.8 Use mathematics in all aspects of scientific inquiry			
Inquiry 5-8.8.1 Use mathematics to structure questions and explanations			
Inquiry 5-8.8.2 Use mathematics to gather, organize, and present data	0%	0%	2.0% (1)
Inquiry 5-8.8.3 Use mathematics to answer questions	8.2% (8)	13.4% (15)	4.0% (2)

So how one test defines inquiry is not how another defines inquiry, as the test questions are addressing different areas of inquiry in different ways. For teachers and administrators, it is important to understand how specific test questions are coded (i.e., for inquiry) and what a score on that coded area actually means. Based on the research cited here, we will flesh out two strategies later on in Chapter 6: learn to analyze curriculum materials and align assessment to curriculum.

THE BOWE AND KINGSBURY STUDY: STATE CUT SCORES VARY GREATLY WHEN COMPARED TO EACH OTHER; STATE ASSESSMENTS ARE NOT AT THE SAME LEVEL OF DIFFICULTY—PURPOSE AND APPROACH

The No Child Left Behind (NCLB) act requires that by 2014 all students be proficient in reading and math. The act requires that states develop tests and establish cut scores indicating proficiency. Is a passing score in one state equivalent to a passing score in another state?

Bowe and Kingsbury (2007) tested 9,000 to 36,000 students per state in Arizona, Colorado, Michigan, and New Hampshire with the Northwest Evaluation Association's (NWEA) RIT assessment. The students also took the state assessment. Bowe and Kingsbury then compared students' scores on the state tests with their scores on the NWEA RIT.

Findings

The following chart (Figure 4.10) shows the variability of the cut scores of the four states. These conclusions could be made because the test

Figure 4.10 Comparison of State Test Proficiency Cut Scores by NWEA Percentile

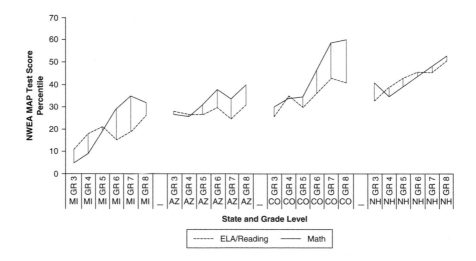

that all the students in the four states took allowed a look at the alignment between state cut scores.

THE NATIONAL CENTER FOR EDUCATIONAL STATISTICS STUDY (2007): STATES VARY GREATLY WHEN THEIR CUT SCORES ON STATE PROFICIENCY TESTS ARE COMPARED WITH THE CUT SCORES ON THE NAEP—PURPOSE AND APPROACH

The National Center for Educational Statistics conducted a study that compared the cut scores on the NAEP with the cut scores for state tests.

Findings

The results are provided in Figure 4.11.

The NAEP proficient cut score is 238 and the basic cut scores is 209. Mapping or aligning the state cut scores shows that all of them are below the proficiency scores required by the NAEP. The chart shows that students reaching proficiency in various states are at different levels of performance. All states are expected to set their own standards for proficiency (which they have done). According to NCLB legislation, all students are expected to reach proficiency by 2014; this means that some state's standards are not as rigorous as others.

Figure 4.11   NAEP Score Equivalents of States' Proficiency Standards for Reading, Grade 4, 2005

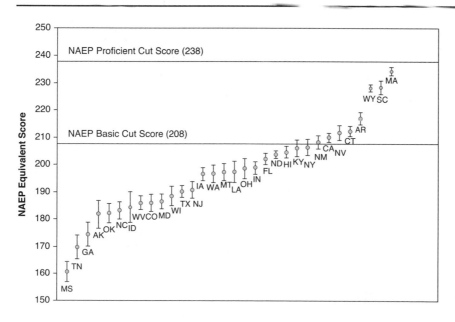

ENGLISH AND STEFFY: BACKLOADING THE CURRICULUM TO ENSURE COVERAGE OF STATE TESTS—PURPOSE AND APPROACH

English and Steffy (2001) suggest a number of ways to align curriculum and instruction to state tests. They suggest "frontloading" the curriculum, which "refers to the practice of creating alignment by physical creation of a curriculum on paper (p. 59), and aligning the curriculum to the appropriate tests. This process follows three phases: preparatory work, writing the curriculum, and piloting the curriculum. Another way to align curriculum is by "backloading" or "beginning the alignment process by working with publicly released test items from the assessment tool" (English & Steffy, 2001, p. 60). Backloading includes seven steps:

- Backloading from public, randomly released test items
- Deconstructing public, randomly released test items
- Developing alternative test items
- Identifying test item distractors
- Examining test to textbook alignment
- Determining written curriculum to test alignment
- Anticipating where the test is moving (English & Steffy, 2001, pp. 98–110)

Findings

English and Steffy do not provide any research that has been directly done to validate this process in schools or school systems. They do quote the Price-Baugh study (1997) and the Moss-Mitchell study (1998) as supporting their process. The English and Steffy study is included here because the work has become so popular in the field, although it focuses on only three sections of the alignment matrix (tests, curriculum, and textbooks) and has no research base for validating this process.

SUMMARY OF FINDINGS FOR STUDIES OF ALIGNMENT OF STATE TESTS

Much of the research in this area focuses on the alignment between state assessments and state standards. As the standards usually are voluminous in comparison to the areas tested, practitioners need to understand the relationship between what is encompassed in the standards and what is actually tested. We also know that the difficulty of state tests vary, so comparison of scores or levels of achievement on state tests is difficult and also calls into question the NCLB legislation that mandates that by 2014 all children need to pass state assessments. There is little research cited in this chapter linking state assessments to district assessments or district instructional practices.

WHAT DISTRICTS CAN DO

#4–1

Lobby the state to provide adequate information on standards and assessments.

Determining alignment between the state standards and the state tests can be difficult because not all states provide the needed and necessary information. For example, some states don't publish test specifications or blueprints. Others substitute released editions of previous tests for test specifications. Some states insist that the standards adequately specify what is on the test. In some states the standards themselves are so general that almost anything might be on the test. States become secretive to preserve the validity and reliability of the test, particularly if the same test is designed to be used year after year (see Popham, 2001, and Squires, 2005a, for more in-depth discussion on the conundrum of standardized testing). As we have previously noted, the standards may include most everything of what students should be able to know and do, and the standards are more comprehensive than the test. It is important for school districts to know what is in the standards and how these are tested (or not tested) on the state test, so districts can make appropriate decisions about what they will teach.

What should states provide to local school districts? From work across the country with many local districts that face this problem, we have put together a list of what states should provide local districts. Additional information has been added using the work of Marca, Redfield, and Winter (2001) which suggested content match, depth match, emphasis, performance match, accessibility, and reporting as six areas to address with alignments of state standards to state assessments. General considerations, not specific procedures, for alignment were enumerated in this reference. Content match is the alignment of the content of state standards to the content of state assessment items. Depth match means aligning the cognitive complexity, or the concept difficulty, between the standards and the assessments. Emphasis means that the emphasis in the assessment should match the emphasis in the standard. Performance match means that the assessment results can be mapped onto the performance levels intended. Accessibility means that all students, even those with disabilities, are able to demonstrate content mastery and that the assessment is free from bias. Reporting means that the assessment reports should be aligned with the standards. It is hoped that where states do not provide this information, districts will lobby the state to improve the state's practice in these areas. Many of these suggestions are also listed in Rabinowitz,

Roeber, Schroeder, and Sheinker (2006). The following list is given using information from the Connecticut State Department of Education as an example.

A. Standards Lists

All states but one (Iowa) have lists of standards by subject area. For reading/language arts, mathematics, social studies, and science—areas that will eventually be tested because of NCLB requirements—districts will want to compare the standards to the test specifications. Figure 4.12 shows the standards for Connecticut.

B. Test Specifications

The state should provide local districts with a listing of the content tested and the number of items associated with each content area. This information should use the same titles as those used in the standards.

The first thing to notice in Figure 4.13 is the titles of the tested areas are not the same as the titles for the standards (see Figure 4.12). This means that the test specifications and the standards are out of alignment.

Figure 4.12   Excerpt of Connecticut Standards for Math K–4

Number Sense	
1.01	Use real-life experiences, physical materials, and technology to construct meanings for whole numbers, commonly used fractions, and decimals.
1.02	Understand our numeration system by modeling, counting, grouping, and using place-value concepts.
1.03	Use numbers to count, as measures, labels, and as indicators of location.
1.04	Use models and pictures to demonstrate understanding of equivalent forms of number.
1.05	Understand and use properties of numbers, including odd, even, ordinal, and cardinal.
1.06	Develop a sense of magnitude of numbers by ordering and comparing whole numbers, commonly used fractions, decimals, and money amounts
Operations	
2.01	Develop meaning for the operations by modeling, comparing, and discussing a variety of problem situations.
2.02	Develop proficiency with basic addition, subtraction, multiplication, and division facts through the use of a variety of strategies and contexts.
2.03	Use informal language, mathematical language, and symbols to relate problem situations to operations.
2.04	Recognize that any one operation can be used to represent diverse problem situations, e.g., subtraction can be used to "take away," as well as compare situations.
2.05	Construct, use, and explain a variety of procedures for performing whole number calculations.
2.06	Understand and use relationships among operations, e.g., multiplication is repetitive addition; multiplication is the opposite of division.

Figure 4.13   Connecticut Mathematics Grade 4 Test Blueprint

Content Standards and Strands	Number of Multiple-Choice Items	Number of Open-Ended Items
Numerical and Proportional Reasoning		
1. Place Value	6	
2. Pictorial Representations of Numbers	4	2
3. Equivalent Fractions, Decimals, and Percents	4	
4. Order, Magnitude, and Rounding of Numbers	6	
5. Models for Operations	4	2
6. Basic Facts	6	
7. Computation With Whole Numbers and Decimals	6	
8. Computation With Fractions and Integers	4	
9. Solve Word Problems	4	
10. Numerical Estimation Strategies	4	
11. Estimating Solutions to Problems	4	
12. Ratios and Proportions	NT	NT
13. Computation With Percents	NT	NT
Geometry and Measurement		
14. Time	4	
15. Approximating Measures	6	
16. Customary and Metric Measures	2	2
17. Geometric Shapes and Properties	2	2
18. Spatial Relationships	NT	NT
Working With Data: Probability and Statistics		
19. Tables, Graphs, and Charts	2	2
20. Statistics and Data Analysis	NT	NT
21. Probability	4	
24. Classification and Logical Reasoning	2	2
Algebraic Reasoning: Patterns and Functions		
22. Patterns	2	2
23. Algebraic Concepts	4	
Integrated Understandings		
25. Mathematical Applications	2	
TOTAL	**80**	**16**
* NT = Strand not tested at this grade level.		

Further, it is not clear how the test specifications map (or are aligned to) the standards, although reasonable guesses can be made.

Notice that the number of items is given for each area, with areas not tested indicated. Also, the number of open-ended items is given for specific areas, such as customary and metric measures. This level of information does not happen in all states.

Further information is available that indicates the sub-areas for each of the tested areas, allowing school districts to know approximately what will be assessed.

Figure 4.14 Connecticut Mastery Test Grade 4 Mathematics Content

Strand	Grade 4 Concepts/Skills Assessed
1. Place Value	A. Solve problems involving 10 MORE/LESS or 100 MORE/LESS than a given number.
	B. Identify alternative forms of expressing whole numbers <1000 using expanded notation.
	C. Identify alternative forms of expressing whole numbers <1000 using regrouping.
	D. Use place value concepts to identify and compare the magnitude and value of digits in 2- and 3-digit numbers.
2. Pictorial Representation of Numbers	A. Relate fractions and decimals to pictorial representations and vice versa.
	B. Relate fractions of regions and sets to pictures and vice versa.
	C. Label and/or shade fractional parts of regions and/or sets.
3. Equivalent Fractions, Decimals, and Percents	A. Relate equivalent fractions to pictorial representations.
4. Order, Magnitude, and Rounding of Numbers	A. Order whole numbers <10,000.
	B. Describe magnitude of 2- and 3-digit whole numbers, fractions, mixed numbers, and decimals (tenths).
	C. Round 2- and 3-digit whole numbers, in context.
	D. Identify points representing 2- and 3-digit whole numbers, fractions (halves, thirds, fourths), and decimals (tenths) on a number line and vice versa.

Strand	Grade 4 Concepts/Skills Assessed
5. Models for Operations	A. Identify members of multiplication and division fact families from arrays (factors of 2, 3, 4, 5, and 10).
	B. Identify the appropriate operation or number sentence to solve a story problem (2-digit numbers).
	C. Write a story problem that matches a given addition, subtraction, or multiplication sentence. Use 1- and 2-digit numbers for addition and subtraction. Use 1-digit factors for multiplication.
6. Basic Facts	A. Find the missing product in a multiplication equation where one factor is 2, 3, 4, 5, or 10.
	B. Find the missing factor in a division equation where one factor is 2, 3, 4, 5, or 10.
7. Computation With Whole Numbers and Decimals	A. Add and subtract 2- and 3-digit whole numbers and money amounts less than $10 with and without regrouping.
	B. Multiply and divide 2-digit whole numbers by one digit.
8. Computation With Fractions and Integers	A. Add and subtract fractions with like denominators.
9. Solve Word Problems	A. Solve one-step story problems involving whole numbers and money amounts. Use 2- and 3-digit numbers in addition and subtraction problems. Use 1- and 2-digit numbers in multiplication problems.
	B. Solve one-step story problems involving addition or subtraction with extraneous information. Use 2-and 3-digit numbers in addition and subtraction problems.
10. Numerical Estimation Strategies	A. Identify the best expression to find an estimate.
11. Estimating Solutions to Problems	A. Identify a reasonable estimate to a problem, including estimating change from $1, $5, and $10.
12. Ratios and Proportions	Not tested

C. Sample Items for Each Area Tested

The sample items should be representative of how questions will be asked and how the answers will be formatted.

Note that each area tested has representative sample items. These sample items are important because they show how students will be required to demonstrate their knowledge. For example, in pictorial representation of numbers, we know from the sample item that students will have to represent equivalence in decimal nomenclature, given the equivalence of one section, and then apply it to many. This may or may not be covered in textbook examples of equivalence, yet students will need to be able to demonstrate their pictorial representation of numbers (decimals) in this way. If students are not given practice on this format, they may know the information but may not be able to demonstrate it in this context.

D. Test Reports Should Give Data for Each Area Listed in the Test Specifications

Figure 4.16 is a test report for Connecticut. The content strands are listed in the first column with the criteria for mastery. The next columns contain individual student scores. The content strands should be consistent with the test specifications or blueprints. In this case the test specifications and the report form have some inconsistencies.

Some states give no feedback by strand, and they only give a total score which then may be aggregated into four or five areas, such as Advanced, At Goal, Proficient, Basic, and Below Basic. Without scores reported by

Figure 4.15   Grade 4 Sample Items for the Connecticut Mastery Test

---

Grade 4 Sample Items

1. Place Value - MC

A store had 375 customers last week. This week, there were 100 more customers than last week. How many customers visited the store this week?

○ 275
○ 365
○ 455
◉ 475

2. Pictorial Representations of Numbers - MC

The shaded part of this figure shows which decimal?

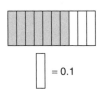

= 0.1

○ 0.73
○ 0.37
◉ 0.7
○ 0.3

3. Pictorial Representations of Numbers - OE

Shade in $1\frac{2}{5}$ of this set of shapes

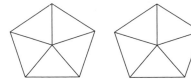

strand, there is no way to know what needs to be improved. If states just report in the four or five areas, their tests may not have enough items to ensure that they can validly and reliably report on student performance by strand. This lack of information for districts will hamper districts' ability to change their programs based on test results. Knowing that 20% of your students scored in the below basic level is not the same as knowing that the district or school was deficient in a skill such as estimating solutions to problems. Some states still opt for this lack of information because the test is cheaper to design and the reports are easier to produce. Let's hope districts will be successful in putting pressure on states to produce tests that yield information that districts can use to improve programs.

Now that we have criteria for states to use in delivering information about tests and standards, let's look at the next strategies districts can use to make sure they have accounted for alignment between the test and other areas on the alignment matrix.

#4–2

Examine the alignment between the standards, the test specifications, and the reports generated by the test.

For districts, it is important to complete the "crosswalk" between the standards, the test specifications, and the test report so the district will know what is being assessed and can make the necessary adjustments. Of

Figure 4.16 Connecticut Mathematics Diagnostic Report for a Sample Teacher

Connecticut Mastery Test
Third Generation

Diagnostic Report

Teacher: BROOKS

Grade: **4**

Simulated Data

MATHEMATICS

Content Strands	Mastery Criteria	CHAN, ROBERT W	CRUZ, ROB Q	DE NIRO, RENEE R	DEPP, PENNY	DUNST, NICK	FOSTER, KRISTER	GRANT, KIRSTEN J	HARRIS, KEANU L	LAW, JULIA A
NUMBER SENSE										
1. Place Value	4 of 6	5	3**	6		5				
2. Pictorial Representations of Numbers	4 of 6	5	2**	5		5				
4. Order, Magnitude and Rounding of Numbers	4 of 6	4	4	4		4				
OPERATIONS										
5. Models for Operations	6 of 8	3**	6	6		3**				
6. Basic Facts	4 of 6	5	1**	4		5				
7. Computation with Whole Numbers and Decimals	4 of 6	6	2**	6		6				
9. Solve Word Problems	4 of 6	6	7	7		6				
ESTIMATION AND APPROXIMATION										
10. Numerical Estimation Strategies	3 of 4	6	6	5		6				
11. Estimating Solutions to Problems	3 of 4	4	4	4		4				
MEASUREMENT										
14. Time	4 of 6	2**	2**	4		2**				
15. Approximating Measures	4 of 6	0**	3**	1**		0**				
16. Customary and Metric Measures	4 of 6	3**	1**	4		3**				
SPATIAL RELATIONSHIPS AND GEOMETRY										
17. Geometric Shapes and Properties	4 of 6	8	3**	8		8				
PROBABILITY AND STATISTICS										
19. Tables, Graphs and Charts	6 of 8	7	4**	7		7				
21. Probability	3 of 4	6	8	7		6				
PATTERNS										
22. Patterns	4 of 6	3**	3**	3**		3**				
DISCRETE MATHEMATICS										
24. Classification and Logical Reasoning	4 of 6	4	3**	6		4				
INTEGRATED UNDERSTANDINGS										
25. Mathematical Applications	4 of 6	2**	3**	4		2**				

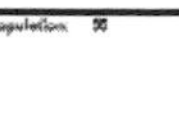

Total student population: 56

Form: O

Test Date: 09/15/04

course, the necessary adjustments will depend on the curriculum design of the district's curriculum. This exercise might also be combined with strategy #2-4 [Provide teachers with opportunities to refine the scope and sequence of courses (especially for science lecture and lab activities), taking into account problematic areas of standards.] so that the district can see whether the practice provided by the textbook reinforces how the item will be tested by the state. This then will examine the alignment encompassing the standards, the test specifications or blueprints, the test reports, and the practice provided in the textbooks.

Pluses

- This will allow the group doing the analysis an in-depth examination of the match between the standards and the state assessment.

Other Considerations

- For this information to be useful, it will need to be shared with staff or with the committees in charge of developing subject area curriculum. Both take time, resources, and staff development planning.

#4–3

State professional organizations could replicate Webb's study using the WAT (Web Alignment Tool) and publish the results.

The full text of Webb's study and the training manual (see http://www.wcer.wisc.edu/WAT/index.aspx) provide enough details that a professional association or state education agency could replicate the study. This would involve training a cadre of educators to validly and reliably judge the alignment between the state test and the state standards. Publication of the results would benefit all districts in the state, because it would spare each having to do a separate analysis of the alignment between the state test and the state standards. Such a process could also yield information that could improve the state's standards and assessments. A national entity like the Association for Supervision and Curriculum Development (ASCD), National School Boards, or the Council of Chief State School Officers could develop a training program to replicate Webb's study in individual states. This would save each state from translating Webb's process for their individual state.

Pluses

- Because Webb provides a validated way to examine the alignment between standards and assessments, this would be a time-efficient way to access the alignment information for the entire state, at relatively little cost depending on how it was implemented.

Other Considerations

- States and professional organizations may be unwilling or unable to conduct such an alignment study.
- The state may not want this information to be generally known or made public because it may point to areas of the standards where no alignment exists with the state test.

#4–4

School districts should require schools to use state testing data to plan improvements.

Again, the power of this recommendation will depend on the design of the curriculum or program in your school district. A school district with no curriculum or program that is instead using textbooks to structure the curriculum will have a different experience from one that has designed assured performances that all students will be challenged to demonstrate.

There are three ways to generate recommendations for improvement using test data: bottom up, top down, and middle out. The bottom up strategy starts with the teacher, then the school, and then the district to synthesize recommendations at each level. The top down strategy starts with district data, then moves to school data, and finally works down to the teacher level. The middle out strategy recognizes the importance of school-based staff development and begins at the school level where goals are set on the basis of testing data; then it progresses either down to the individual teacher level or up through aggregating school data into district recommendations. If there is consistency in the data across the district, a top down approach may work the best. A bottom up approach may be appropriate if there is great variation among schools. The middle out approach could be used if the other two are inappropriate.

Whatever strategy is used, each level produces a strengths and needs analysis based on the report of test scores. Teachers then examine the school-level report, meet as a group, and come to consensus on the strengths and needs the data show in the report (see Figure 4.17). Next, the strengths and needs are put together in a staff development plan for the school that will show how the needs will be addressed. Grade-level meetings and faculty meetings are two times where this work can be accomplished without having to use districtwide staff development days. Grade-level or course teachers can be released for a half day through hiring substitutes and cycling a number of grade-level or course teachers through this cycle (see Figure 4.18).

If the textbook provides the basis for the program, teachers will have more work to do because they will have to figure out when and how a particular topic is taught. Then they will need to discuss their own strengths and weaknesses on teaching the topic. Next, they will come up with a plan for their own staff development. Finally, they can use students' results on next year's tests as a way to evaluate whether their staff development was successful. If students score better, then the assumption can be made that the staff development was a success.

If teachers have developed a curriculum where all teach particular assured activities, then the previous work of generating those activities makes easier work of analyzing scores and generating staff development plans. For example, suppose that the district reports show a weakness in a particular area. Representative teachers from across the district meet and review the assured activities that are used to teach this concept. Obviously, the scope and sequence of the assured activities needs to be revised because students aren't performing well on the test. Some new assured activities may be added, others modified or discarded. Then the representative teachers share their consensus recommendations with their schools. After modifications, a new scope and sequence of assured activities are used during the next school year. Staff development time is proposed for all who need a chance to practice the new assured activities before they are actually used in the classroom. Again, student performance on the state test in this concept domain is the way the teachers evaluate their curriculum and staff development efforts.

From this one example, it is clear that the design of curriculum in the district will either facilitate a yearly rational response to high-stakes test results or it will interfere with the effectiveness of interventions.

Pluses

- Testing information, including the district's strengths and needs, is fed back into staff and curriculum development, ensuring that the following year's plans are in sync with the most recent testing data.
- There is a systematic process for developing staff and curriculum needs based on current testing data.

Figure 4.17   Strengths and Needs Work Sheet Based on State Assessment Data

Grade Level _____

School _____

Strengths	Needs

Figure 4.18   Strengths and Needs Analysis Leads to Staff Development Planning
Work Sheet

Grade Level _____

School _____

Staff Development Activity	Date/Time	Addresses Need	Eval Collected

- School improvement can be tied to the most recent testing data while at the same time addressing the general needs of the district.

Other Considerations

- Time and resources are needed to tackle this intervention. Processes need to be developed and implemented that will allow meeting the needs of both the district and the schools for improvement.

#4–5

Set multiyear goals for district performance on state tests.

One school district, which will remain nameless, examined their previous test scores and the improvement or lack of improvement from year to year in order to determine areas that needed priority considerations from a district perspective.

In the first column of Figure 4.19 are listed the tests (currently given in Grades 4, 6, 8, and 10 for reading, writing, and math, and given in Grade 10 for science). The second column shows the percentage gain or loss using the year 2000 as a base and examining the cumulative gain or loss over the last four years. The third column shows where the school district is now, according to their state report card. The fourth column says that all students will need to reach 100% by 2014. By subtracting 100% needed by 2014 from the percentage of students currently meeting goal, the district can establish the needed growth for the next ten years. For example, in fourth-grade reading, the current percentage of students meeting goal for the district is 68.3%. The growth needed in the next ten years is 31.7% (100% needed in 2014 minus current percentage meeting goal equals 31.7%). The next to the last column shows the progress needed per year (3.2% more each year for the next ten years to make goal for fourth-grade reading). The column "Avr. yearly progress 2000–2004" shows the "% gain or loss 2000–2004" from the first column divided by the three years of data represented. For example, scores declined from 2000 to 2004 by 2.7%, resulting in an average yearly progress of –9%. By comparing the trend (–9%) with the needed improvement per year, based on the existing performance (3.2%), we see in the last column that if current progress continues, the district will not make its goal by 2014.

Generally for the district as a whole, the most improvement needed on a yearly basis is 4.4% more students scoring in the proficient category or higher compared with the previous year. The least amount of improvement needed is 1.6% improvement each year. One hundred percent proficiency can be achieved if stretched out over the long-term. But, as Figure 4.19

Figure 4.19   Work Sheet for Computing Annual Progress Needed to Meet the Needs of NCLB

	% Gain or Loss 2000-04	Current % Meeting Goal 2004	% Needed by 2014	Growth Needed in Next 10 Years	Average Yearly Progress 2000–04	Average Yearly Progress Needed to Meet Goal in 2014	"–" Current Progress is Not Enough; "+" Current Progress, if Maintained, is Enough
4-r	(2.7)	68.3	100	31.7	(0.9)	3.2	—
4-w	7.0	76.1	100	23.9	2.3	2.4	—
4-m	(0.3)	68.7	100	31.3	(0.1)	3.1	—
all 3	8.0	55.6	100	44.4	2.7	4.4	—
6-r	3.7	79.7	100	20.3	1.2	2.0	—
6-w	11.8	79.6	100	20.4	3.9	2.0	+
6-m	9.8	77.8	100	22.2	3.3	2.2	+
all 3	9.8	62	100	38	3.3	3.8	—
8-r	0.1	84.1	100	15.9	0.0	1.6	—
8-w	8.4	81.4	100	18.6	2.8	1.9	+
8-m	0.9	66.9	100	33.1	0.3	3.3	—
all 3	3.9	57.8	100	42.2	1.3	4.2	—
10-r	18.8	60.8	100	39.2	6.3	3.9	+
10-w	13.4	60.4	100	39.6	4.5	4.0	+
10-m	1.6	57.6	100	42.4	0.5	4.2	—
10-s	23.2	61.2	100	38.8	7.7	3.9	+
all 4	15.7	34.2	100	65.8	5.2	6.6	—

NOTE: a. By 2014 we will fail in reading except for 10th grade.

b. By 2014 we will fail in writing except in 6th, 8th, and 10th grade.

c. By 2014 we will fail in math except in 6th grade.

d. By 2014 we will pass science in 10th grade.

e. By 2014 we will fail to get 100% pased all tests.

Therefore, by 2014 we will fail to make annual yearly progress and be declared a failing school district by the state and federal government using the No Child Left Behind Law.

indicates, only about one-third of the subjects at the various grade levels have made estimated progress over the last three years of data (see the last column and notice the + notations.) Although these differences present small concerns now, as 2014 approaches their significance will grow. Given that the data are based on past performance, the trends give one indication if the district can meet the goal of 100% proficient in the next decade.

Pluses

- The district has a systematic way to plan yearly for improvements so that NCLB goals can be met over the long-term.

Other Considerations

- Coordination of effort will be needed between the district and the school so that district and school goals are mutually supporting.
- Time and resources will be needed to systematize how the analysis will be conducted by both district and school, conduct the analysis, and use the data to develop school and district improvement plans.

#4–6

Lobby the state to use Achieve's Ten Criteria for Essential Elements of a State's Longitudinal Data System.
The ten criteria are:

1. A unique statewide student identifier.

2. Student-level enrollment, demographic, and program participation information.

3. The ability to match individual students' test records from year to year to measure academic growth.

4. Information on untested students.

5. A teacher identifier system with the ability to match teachers to students.

6. Student-level transcript information, including information on courses completed and grades earned.

7. Student-level college readiness test scores.

8. Student-level graduation and dropout data.

9. The ability to match student records between the pre-K–12 and postsecondary systems.

10. A state data audit system assessing data quality, validity, and reliability. (Achieve, http://www.achieve.org/dstore.nsf/Lookup/ DQC_paper/$file/DQC_paper.pdf, retrieved March 3, 2006)

Pluses

Such standards for a state would make it possible to

- follow students' academic progress as they move from grade to grade;
- determine the value-added efficiencies of specific schools and programs;
- identify consistently high-performing schools so that educators and the public can learn from best practices;
- evaluate the effect of teacher preparation and training programs on student achievement;
- focus school systems on preparing a higher percentage of students to succeed in rigorous high school courses, college, and challenging jobs.

Given that it will take a few years to make such changes, particularly at the state level, districts can begin to adopt data structures that will allow them to use the information from state tests and their own curriculum alignment strategies to structure data and implement data-mining strategies that will provide partial answers to questions of how to improve student achievement.

Other Considerations

- States will be resistant to changing the way data is reported.
- Data systems that meet these criteria are more expensive than systems that don't. Resources will be a continuing problem.

#4–7

Backload the curriculum: Align released test items with curriculum and textbooks.

Using English and Steffy's (2001) process, backload the curriculum to ensure alignment of curriculum, state tests, and textbooks.

Pluses

- Backloading ensures a curriculum that covers the content of state tests.

Other Considerations

- Backloading the curriculum will narrow the curriculum to just the content that is tested on a state's tests. State tests assess a rather narrow range of content when a complete list of standards is considered; thus key concepts and processes may be left out of the curriculum.

Part II

Alignment and Mastery Learning, Project 2061, and TIMSS

In Part I we .reviewed individual studies that generally related one facet of the alignment matrix to another, such as studies that related instruction to curriculum-embedded tests. In Part II we will examine research that deals with multiple areas of the alignment matrix at once. For example, some of the research on mastery learning encompasses instruction, curriculum-embedded assessments, and standardized tests. The ideas are more complex because they involve pieces of the alignment matrix which are interdependent. Yet within this complexity there is power, as the research for the three areas suggests achievement can be improved. Such research suggests that a systematic approach to alignment may be the best way to address alignment issues

Alignment, Reteaching, and Mastery Learning

A PERSONAL NOTE

You may well ask, "What is mastery learning, an instructional model from the 1980s, doing in a contemporary book about alignment?" The answer comes from my decade of experience implementing mastery learning in a New Jersey school district and seeing performance go from below grade level to above grade level on standardized tests. The mastery learning model requires districts to align their curriculum and instruction with curriculum-embedded tests and standardized tests. Here are the details of my experience.

The district served mainly poor and minority students. When we started mastery learning, there were very few examples out there to learn from. My job as curriculum director in the district was to put the mastery learning model in place with the assistance of all the teachers and administrators. About seven years into the process, a woman by the name of Kathleen Wishnick, did her dissertation on the results in Red Bank, New Jersey. She compared results of unit assessments with the results of the standardized test we were using (this was before state tests had come along). She found that when the unit tests were not aligned to the standardized test, socioeconomic status, teacher, and gender largely predicted the results on the standardized test. Much other research has been done since that supports this finding. In some ways, this was what we expected.

What was startling—and the reason this book is being written today—is that when the unit tests were aligned to the standardized tests, students' socioeconomic status, teacher, and gender fell out of the equation for predicting student achievement. This means that these usually controlling variables had very little influence on the results—that aligned instruction can overcome socioeconomic status, teacher, and gender influences. This is huge! Student achievement no longer needs to depend on factors like socioeconomic status and gender. It really is possible to design an instructional system where all children learn in spite of their backgrounds or socioeconomic status.

The second reason I emphasize mastery learning is because of a recent review of literature that I did for Edvantia in Charleston, West Virginia, one of fourteen educational labs around the country funded by the U.S. government (Squires, 2005c). The review looked at research on students who received feedback during instruction, part of the mastery learning model. Even I was impressed by the consistency and the power of the results. Students that received feedback did better on tests that were aligned with the instruction, whether in a mastery learning model or another instructional situation.

I think those messages are too powerful to ignore and they reinforce the contention of this book that alignment is an important element of districts' curriculum development processes.

INTRODUCTION

Mastery learning, a powerful idea introduced in the 1970s, gained attention of school districts around the country in the 1980s. This model and its validation in laboratory settings was adopted and applied in school settings with many successes (Block, Efthim, & Burns, 1989). In this chapter we examine the mastery learning model, showing how it ties into alignment practices; investigate its application and research validation in one school district; and then pursue Cohen's (1987) ideas that alignment may have been responsible for the power of the mastery learning results. The chapter ends with a number of practices for school districts that are suggested by this part of the review of the alignment research.

BLOOM'S THEORY OF SCHOOL LEARNING—PURPOSE AND APPROACH

Based in part on Carroll's model (1963), Bloom (1976) provides a testable theory of school learning. Bloom wanted to "determine a small number of variables which will account for much of the variation in school learning." The quest to understand student achievement continues today. Bloom proposed three interdependent variables:

- Cognitive Entry Behaviors: the extent to which the student has already learned the basic prerequisites of the learning to be accomplished
- Affective Entry Characteristics: the extent to which the student is (or can be) motivated to engage in the learning process
- Quality of Instruction: the extent to which the instruction to be given is appropriate to the learner (Bloom, 1976, pp. 10–11).

Instruction is defined by "learning tasks." Quality of instruction, incorporated in learning tasks, includes the extent to which the cues, practice, and reinforcement of the learning are appropriate to the needs of the learner. The entry characteristics and behaviors of students along with quality of instruction yield three learning outcomes: level and type of achievement, the rate of learning, and affective outcomes.

Where the student entry characteristics and the quality of instruction are favorable, then all the learning outcomes will be at a high or positive level and there should be little variation in the measures of the outcomes. Where there is considerable variation among students in their entry characteristics and where the quality of instruction is not optimal for the different students, there should be great variation in the learning outcomes" (Bloom, 1976, pp. 11–12).

These ideas were revolutionary at the time, as Bloom believed that a scope and sequence of learning tasks could be designed so higher learning

Figure 5.1   Bloom's Model of Instructional Quality

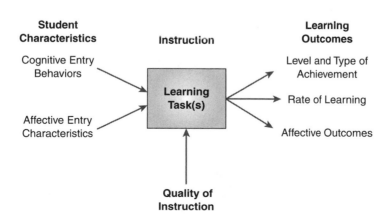

outcomes were ensured for all students, not just some students. Quality of instruction could make up for deficits in cognitive and affective entry behaviors of students and districts control the quality of instruction.

Bloom believed that modifications are possible in students' prerequisites and motivations for learning and that modifications in the quality of instruction could improve student outcomes. Specifically, if instructional quality improves, student outcomes improve. If student outcomes improve, then students are better prepared cognitively and affectively for the next sequence of instructional tasks. Bloom's theory emphasized that the scope and sequence of instructional tasks—the curriculum—will make a difference in students' performances. "The quality of instruction students receive has a demonstrable effect on their achievement and learning processes over one or more learning tasks" (Bloom, 1976, p. 171).

Additionally, if students have appropriate prerequisite skills, any developmentally appropriate learning task can be learned. This implies that while family and socioeconomic status may initially correlate with student entry behaviors and affective characteristics and determine student outcomes to a great extent, the school can design curriculum (a series of learning tasks) that can assist students in mastering the curriculum, and thereby change over time student entry behaviors and affective characteristics for subsequent learning tasks. Put in today's parlance, "All students can reach high standards." (See Gentile and Lalley, 2003, for a book-length discussion of mastery learning and how it can be used to increase student performance with standards.)

A critical step for quality instruction required providing a teach, test, reteach, test model. Teachers would use the results of a formative test to provide students who didn't master the learning task with more and different instruction. Then all students would validate mastery after the reteaching time. By using the formative tests as the criteria for providing additional instruction, teachers ensure that more students master the learning task. As more students master the previous learning tasks, more students are ready for the subsequent learning tasks. And the subsequent learning tasks take less time because more students have the appropriate prerequisite skills. (See Squires, 2005c, for a review of relevant literature.) Bloom (1976) validated this theory using different student populations, different learning tasks, and different subject matter (see Arlin, 1973; Binor, 1974; Block, 1970; and Levin, 1975, for examples).

Findings

Based on his research, Bloom (1976) concluded that feedback and corrective procedures account for 25% of the variation in student learning. Although Bloom focused on individual students instead of classrooms, schools, or school systems, his theory suggests that schools and classroom teachers who provide consistent feedback on instruction to low performers could achieve better results.

Indeed, in further reviews of mastery learning research, Block (1971, 1974) and Block and Burns (1976) reviewed numerous studies which indicated that mastery learning is successful at raising achievement levels of approximately 80% of students to the high levels now enjoyed by only 20% of students. In these reviews, effect sizes ranged from .5 to over 1.5. Block et al. (1989) reviewed forty-eight studies of mastery learning and concluded:

> Mastery learning approaches seem to work comparatively well almost all of the time. That is, they typically produce effects that are greater than or equal to a non-mastery approach. . . . Mastery learning approaches have comparatively strong effects on general student achievement. Assuming normality of scores, a median effect size of .76 [from the 48 studies] means that the typical application should move the average 50th percentile student to about the 77th percentile in achievement. (p. 28)

More reviews (Gentile & Lalley, 2003; Guskey & Pigott, 1988; Kulik, Kulik, & Bangert-Drowns, 1990; Stallings and Stipek, 1986) continued finding effects on achievement and also effects on teachers' attitudes and perceptions of students, increased retention of learned information, and students' perceptions of confidence in their own abilities.

The research we've just discussed demonstrates that the theory behind the model could be successfully applied in schools and school districts. But districts and schools who adopted Bloom's model generally had to change the structure of curriculum, the delivery of instruction, and the function of the assessment system in order to get these results—no small task. Let's examine the implications.

Gentile and Lalley (2003) provide a description of three common elements of any mastery learning system:

1. Explicit instructional objectives, hierarchically sequenced, which students are expected to obtain [curriculum structure]

2. Criterion-referenced assessment to evaluate and provide feedback on the achievement of those objectives [assessment system]

3. Remedial instruction for students who did not achieve the desired standard of performance [instructional delivery] (p. 156)

Based on these characteristics, districts would generally need to make the following changes. The first two common elements—a scope and sequence of instructional objectives and a criterion-referenced assessment system—must be determined on a districtwide basis in order for instruction to make sense across years between grade levels or courses, when students usually change teachers. Most school districts do not have these elements in place, so implementing a mastery learning philosophy means developing districtwide instructional objectives and a criterion-referenced assessment system.

In addition, the scope and sequence and the assessment system would need to be aligned to state standards and assessments in such a way that the district is assured instruction covers the topics in the standards and state assessments.

The Bloom model was based on a series of learning tasks, and success on those learning tasks were prerequisite to other learning tasks. The district or school would need to specify the learning tasks and make sure all students had the opportunity to learn those tasks (based on a scope and sequence of objectives). Remember, back in the 1980s most districts used textbooks for their curriculum, there were no standards, and no required testing or reporting of test results. So specifying the learning tasks associated with a scope and sequence of objectives (a curriculum), and requiring all students to have access to those tasks (which required all teachers to teach those tasks), would drastically change the instructional practices of these districts.

Further, the power of mastery learning resided in teachers providing feedback to students after testing, reteaching students who did not meet mastery, and providing enrichment for those who initially mastered the material. In today's language, we would talk about differentiating instruction. Again, large changes were necessary to implement the model, just as large changes are needed today to implement differentiated instruction. Teachers had to take more time with each task, because they had to reteach after the task for those students who didn't master. More time on current tasks meant less time for future tasks, so teachers couldn't cover the same number of tasks as they might have before. Formative assessments needed to be standardized within districts, so all students took the same formative assessment, posing difficulties in school cultures were every teacher developed and used their own assessments. Teachers needed to develop different ways of teaching the learning task for those who didn't pass the formative assessment, running counter to some existing beliefs that "My job is to teach, assess, and tell students how well they did. Students should pass tests the first time; I don't coddle kids with second chances," or, "I have always taught this way in the past, and kids got it. Now I am required to figure out different ways to reteach." These changes all would require staff development so teachers had the skills and attitudes to fully implement mastery learning.

The laboratory studies that Bloom conducted validated the theory based on individual classrooms of students, but neglected to anticipate the large changes needed in the existing culture of schools and districts to actually implement the process. What the Bloom model showed us is that when curriculum, instruction, and lesson planning are aligned with curriculum-embedded tests (and there is a teach, test, reteach, test model in place), student results can improve dramatically in the laboratory and in schools and school districts that implement the model well (see Levine and associates, 1985, for an example).

This work is placed on the alignment matrix to indicate that Bloom's work demonstrates that when instruction is aligned with curriculum-embedded tests (and students have the opportunity for reteaching on the test's content), student outcomes tend to improve.

Figure 5.2   The Alignment Matrix—Mastery Learning

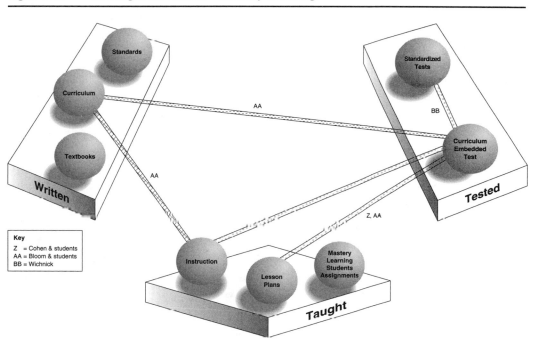

The alignment matrix for mastery learning centers around the alignment of curriculum-embedded tests to the written and taught curriculum. This is the first look at a system of curriculum that has been shown to improve student results.

Bloom's theory of instructional quality implies that the school controls factors that affect student outcomes; outcomes are not predetermined by race, culture, or socioeconomic status, but are under the control of the school. Cohen's (1987) and Wishnick's (1989) work is also placed on the alignment matrix; we will explore their research next.

COHEN: INSTRUCTIONAL ALIGNMENT— PURPOSE AND APPROACH

Cohen's (1987) emphasis was similar to Bloom's in that Cohen's work demonstrated the power of alignment between instruction and the content of curriculum-embedded tests; Cohen coined it "instructional alignment" and focused his studies specifically on the alignment aspects. Bloom's theory, on the other hand, focused on instruction after formative testing. Central to Cohen's ideas is that "Lack of excellence in American schools is not caused by ineffective teaching, but mostly by misaligning what teachers teach, what they intend to teach, and what they assess as having been taught" (Cohen, 1987, p. 18). To buttress the case, Cohen and his graduate students found that misalignment of instruction to testing caused low-aptitude students to fail, while high-aptitude students succeeded.

Findings

When instruction and assessment were aligned during sample lessons, both low- and high-aptitude students scored well on curriculum-embedded tests. Generally, alignment was more important for low-aptitude students than for high-aptitude students, with low-aptitude students making greater gains when alignment is present. When instruction aligns with assessment, large gains over a control group (instruction with no alignment) appeared across studies, with effect sizes ranging around four times what traditional instruction produced (effect sizes ranging from .25 to .50) or for instructionally aligned instruction and assessment, effect sizes of 1 to 2, meaning that a student scoring at a 50 percentile would increase to between 84 and 98 percentile (Cohen & Stover, 1981; Elia, 1986; Fahey, 1986; Kozar, 1984; Tallarico, 1984). This research promised better student results if instruction aligned practice with test items as well as the concepts the items tested, particularly for low-aptitude students.

THE WISHNICK STUDY: ALIGNMENT IS MORE IMPORTANT THAN SOCIOECONOMIC STATUS IN PREDICTING ACHIEVEMENT—PURPOSE AND APPROACH

Wishnick (1989), a student of Cohen's, examined the effect of alignment between curriculum-embedded tests in fourth-grade reading units and a standardized test in Red Bank, New Jersey. Red Bank Public Schools implemented a mastery learning curriculum that had produced improved achievement on standardized tests (Squires, 1986). Wishnick (1989) states the purpose of her study:

> In a mastery learning curriculum, how much of the variance in norm referenced standardized achievement test (NRST) scores is explained by: (1) gender; (2) socioeconomic status (SES); (3) teacher effect; (4) scores on locally developed criterion referenced tests (CRTs) purporting to measure the same skills as what is measured on commercially published normed referenced standardized tests (NRSTs). . . . The study's proposed to investigate the power of instructional alignment compared to the power of demographics that have usually explained significant amounts of NRST scores variance." (pp. 1, 3)

Wishnick concludes by saying, "The study compared the relative potencies of instructional methods with demographic factors" (p. 4). A preponderance of the research has established strong links between a student's socioeconomic status, teacher effect, and gender as predictors of success on norm referenced standardized tests. If the curriculum and assessments are aligned, will this correlation still hold true?

To conduct the study, Wishnick obtained a number of materials and records from Red Bank Public Schools: copies of the curriculum for fourth-grade reading, copies of the criterion referenced tests for each reading unit designed by the district's fourth-grade teachers, logs of students scores on those criterion referenced tests, individual student raw scores for the standardized test along with the copy of the test and testing material, and a record of whether students received free or reduced lunch (an indicator of poverty level).

Wishnick developed and validated an Alignment Measurement Scale (AMS) (See Figure 5.3) that quantified the degree of instructional alignment between the CRT (Criterion Referenced Test) and NRST (Norm Referenced Standardized Test) item clusters. The AMS measured the alignment of the CRT (embedded in the instructional process) with the NRST given near the end of the year. Wishnick identified seventeen critical features that contribute to alignment and converted these into seven subscales. Each subscale could be assigned a range of five values: 4=Positive Misalignment, meaning that the CRT was more difficult than the NRST; 3=Perfect Alignment; 2=Satisfactory Alignment; 1=Poorly Aligned; and 0=Misalignment.

Each item on the scale has a particular meaning that needs to be understood by the person rating the alignment between the CRT and the

Figure 5.3   Wishnick's Alignment Measurement Scale

PERF 1	PERF 2		AMS Total		
Directions: Circle the appropriate score for each item. This Likert scale assigns the following values: 4 = PM Positive Misalignment; 3 = AL Perfect Alignment; 3 = S Satisfactory; 1 = P Poorly Aligned; 0 = MIS Misaligned					
	PM	**AL**	**S**	**P**	**MIS**
SCM Skill Concept Match	4	3	2	1	0
SLM Skill Level Match	4	3	2	1	0
FM Format Match					
Items Look Alike	4	3	2	1	0
*Arrangement of Items	4	3	2	1	0
Length of Stimuli	4	3	2	1	0
*Number of Items (Tasks)	4	3	2	1	0
*Mixture of Items (Tasks)	4	3	2	1	0
DM Directions Match					
Delivery of Instructions	4	3	2	1	0
Format of Directions	4	3	2	1	0
Cue Match					
Types of Response Stimuli	4	3	2	1	0
Hints Within Stimuli	4	3	2	1	0
EM Enticer Match					
Stimulus Response Difference	4	3	2	1	0
*Rule Application Mix	4	3	2	1	0
PCM Performance Conditions Match					
Time Limit	4	3	2	1	0
Press to Perform	4	3	2	1	0
Response Mode	4	3	2	1	0
Teacher Behavior	4	3	2	1	0

SOURCE: Wishnick, K. T. (1989). *Relative effects on achievements scores of SES, gender, teacher effect and instructional alignment: A study of alignment's power in mastery learning.* Unpublished doctoral dissertation, University of San Francisco, CA. © 1989 K. T. Wishnick. Reprinted with permission.

NOTE: *These critical features are only measured when generating an AMS score for an entire test. Do not measure these critical features when measuring alignment of individual items.

NRST. The AMS was applied to item clusters for the CRT and the NRST. Item clusters for both the CRT and NRST were generated based on concept similarity (were the concepts tested similar?) combined with the way the concepts were tested (for example, were the predicting outcomes items phrased positively with the word *could* in the stem?). Item clusters from the

CRT and NRST were then aligned, if similar, and excluded from further analysis if there was no alignment. These clusters were then rated using the AMS instrument after establishing inter-rater reliability and validity of the instrument. The AMS ratings and information about gender, socio-economic status, and teacher were analyzed. (The analysis was complex and beyond the scope easily reported in a small space here.)

Findings

The findings, in a nutshell, are that alignment is more powerful in predicting student achievement than socioeconomic status, gender, or teacher—a stunning finding, given the vast majority of research that shows a strong connection, for example, between socioeconomic status and performance. Here are the findings in more detail; many have been directly quoted or paraphrased from the dissertation.

- Correlations between the CRT and the NRST scores of students were compared with the alignment scores on the AMS. The higher the alignment score on the AMS, the greater the correlations between the CRT and the NRST. Good alignment then tends to reduce the variability of student scores. Poor alignment increases the variability in student scores. (Wishnick, 1989, pp. 135–137)
- Socioeconomic status accounted for only 1% of the NRST performance variance. This means that whether a student received free or reduced lunch had almost nothing to do with how well he or she scored on the NRST. Most research studies have found that students' socioeconomic status is predictive of how well they score on standardized tests. This finding shows that aligned instruction and assessment washes out socioeconomic status as a predictor of achievement. (Wishnick, 1989, pp. 139–141)
- Gender and teacher also accounted for little of the variance in student scores. In other studies the reverse was true. Reading scores for females are generally higher than males at fourth grade. Teachers produce different results, but in this study it did not matter what teacher was assigned to a student; the chances of scoring high were approximately equal across classes studied. Wishnick, 1989, pp. 141–142)
- Taken as a whole, the higher the degree of instructional alignment between the CRT and the NRST, the less effect

demographic variables, gender, socioeconomic status, and teacher had on NRST performance. (Wishnick, 1989, p. 144)

- The lower the degree of instructional alignment between the CRT and NRST item cluster, the higher the degree of influence of demographic variables on NRST performance. (Wishnick, 1989, pp.144–45)

- The alignment effect is more powerful for low achievers than for high achievers. Low achievers do better when the instructional outcomes are clear and instruction is congruent with postinstructional assessment. (Wishnick, 1989, p. 158)

- The CRT was the best predictor of scores on the NRST, better than gender, socioeconomic status, and teacher effect. (Wishnick, 1989, p. 147)

- The power of instruction as measured by the CRT accounted for 40.32% of NRST performance variance, and the alignment effect accounted for 36.72% of NRST performance variance. Taken as a whole, other variables (i.e., gender, teacher effect, and socioeconomic status) accounted for 3% of NRST performance variance. (Wishnick, 1989, p. 154)

- Socioeconomic status is a potent factor in school performance when instruction is generated from a model of education that assumes a normal distribution of scholastic performance. But when the educational model assumes that all students can demonstrate mastery, and when instruction is aligned, students perform well on competency tests and socioeconomic status loses its effect on school performance. Competency-based criterion referenced instruction is more potent than socioeconomic status. (Wishnick, 1989, pp.164–166)

- This study found no evidence to support previous research that teachers interact differently with these fourth-grade students. The simple correlation between teacher and total NRST performance approached zero . . . the lack of teacher effect is the teacher effect in this mastery learning design. (Wishnick, 1989, pp. 167–170)

SUMMARY OF FINDINGS FOR STUDIES OF MASTERY LEARNING

These studies point out the importance of feedback during instruction. In mastery learning this feedback is formally incorporated into the instructional model as the student is retaught using a different approach. In order to have systematic feedback like this, the following need to be in place:

- A scope and sequence of key instructional assessment opportunities
- A standard way of assessing instructional performance
- An alternative way of teaching for those students who don't initially pass the assessment

This provides the beginning of the criteria for a curriculum structure that can produce results.

Alignment, as Wishnick's study pointed out, is important in crafting assessments where there needs to be alignment along various dimensions (defined by the Alignment Management Scale). When alignment is present between curriculum-embedded assessments and state or standardized assessments, traditional variables such as race, socioeconomic status, and teacher assignment fall out of the equation for student performance. This chapter demonstrates that it is possible to design a curriculum that has powerful effects on student performance, negating effects of race, socioeconomic status, and teacher assignment.

WHAT DISTRICTS CAN DO

We discussed some of the difficulties in implementing mastery learning:

- Linking learning tasks (that all students are expected to master) with a scope and sequence aligned to standards
- Developing and providing a criterion-referenced assessment structure including formative and summative assessments
- Providing feedback and reteaching after formative tests as standard operating procedure for a district's teachers

Those difficulties, however, point to things districts might change, given the strength of the research.

#5–1

Implement a mastery learning model districtwide.
This requires a district to develop and use learning tasks that will be the foundation for instruction. For each unit composed of learning tasks, the district needs to develop an assessment system in which each unit has a

formative and summative assessment that tests the content and objectives covered in that unit. The district's instructional model needs to encompass a teach, test, reteach, test model with the accompanying staff development for all teaching staff. Gentile and Lalley (2003) suggest another requirement: "Enrichment activities and a corresponding grading scheme to go beyond initial mastery of essentials to higher-order thinking with application of their newly acquired knowledge and skills" (p. 156). Such a systematic approach may be necessary because in the existing model of instruction and assessment (teach, test), students don't receive appropriate feedback that ensures mastery of specified learning tasks.

Pluses

- This is a systematic, research-based, field-tested approach that encompasses many of the key components needed to raise student achievement.
- Mastery learning has been proven to produce dramatic increases in student achievement in the real world of school districts.

Other Considerations

- There needs to be a large commitment of staff development and program development time to be ready for implementation.
- It is a long time before results can be garnered, during which staff and program development are taking place.
- Many changes will need to be made in the practices of most school districts around linking objectives with learning tasks that all students use, developing formative and summative assessments, and implementing an instructional model that involves reteaching in all classrooms.

Other, less systematic approaches follow.

#5–2

Develop standard ways to periodically assess and reteach students.
One component of mastery learning is a standardized assessment system. Districts can provide an assessment system to help generate data that can be used in the district's data-use efforts. Some districts have developed quarterly assessments or assessments at the end of semesters, and in other districts, particularly in secondary schools, a final examination system is in place, in which all students taking particular courses take the same final exam. These assessments may be aligned to the format of the state tests and mirror the content of the state exams.

Pluses

- Assessment drives instruction, so providing a standard assessment at specific time intervals may create the institutional press to help teachers align more of their activities (learning tasks) to the content and format of the high-stakes tests.
- Students receive practice on an assessment that is aligned with the state test.
- This strategy is relatively easy to add on, as it requires minimal loss of instructional time and can be developed at the central office.
- This strategy creates assessment data, so the results can be fed back into the system to improve curriculum, instruction, and assessment.

Other Considerations

- This emphasizes the standardized test too much.
- The test may not be aligned to what is taught during that time period in the district, an example of not aligning the assessment with the curriculum.
- The district-developed test may have been developed without formal and public test specifications, presenting teachers and students with another mystery test.
- Alignment may be imprecise, based on sample test items rather than on the test specifications themselves.
- This does not ensure that the data will be fed back so that instruction and curriculum can actually be improved, as the district may not have any way of knowing what should be taught in particular courses or grade levels.

#5–3

Provide feedback to students on a regular basis while providing iterative ways for students to demonstrate competence on learning tasks.

The research on mastery learning shows that when students receive feedback and different instructional strategies when they are not mastering a learning task, their performance improves dramatically. This improvement prepares them to better perform on subsequent tasks, because they have had the opportunity to master the subsequent task's prerequisite skills. Using a teach, test, reteach, test instructional model is a staff development effort that could be implemented over the course of a year or two. Coverage expectations would need to be modified so that the extra time needed to complete reteaching would be available, although the research suggests that time needed at the beginning of a course for attention to students not making the grade will be made up later as all students master a course's prerequisite skills.

Pluses

- This strategy provides structure for differentiating instruction after the formative test.
- Students can receive feedback and be taught in a different way, resulting in more students mastering the learning tasks.
- Everyone must demonstrate competence in regrouping based on data.
- Students have more time to demonstrate competence on important fundamentals.
- Compliance can be easily documented in teachers' lesson plans.

Other Considerations

- Without standard assessments, teachers will use personal criteria to determine the need for reteaching.
- Modifying coverage expectations without a curriculum will be problematic.
- Without the support of grade-level or course-level teams and administrative oversight, this may be just another flash-in-the-pan inservice. Districts without the infrastructure to provide follow-up coaching and problem solving will be hard pressed to maintain the model.

Ideas From Project 2061 of the American Association for the Advancement of Science

In Chapter 3, we covered the science and math textbook analysis process and results of Project 2061 of the American Association for the Advancement of Science (AAAS). This chapter covers their work on implementing science standards through curriculum and staff development, one way to merge many of the research-based strategies and capture the power of alignment to affect student achievement.

Project 2061 proposes that many areas of education need to be changed if standards and their assessments are to have an effect. Rather than using a research-based argument in which experimental and control group results are compared, Project 2061 uses a logical and rational analysis of problems confronting [science] education and details strategies for fixing problems over the long-term, hence the project's title "Project 2061," the date when Halley's comet will return to Earth's proximity. Many of the initiative's systematic recommendations involve the alignment of standards, curriculum, instruction, and assessments.

In this chapter we will examine the tools that Project 2061 uses:

- *Science for All Americans* (1989) is a description of what students should know in order to be scientifically literate by the end of their high school education.
- *Benchmarks for Science Literacy* (1993) uses the results of Science for All Americans to develop grade-level (K–2, 3–5, 6–8, and 9–12) bands of what students should know and be able to do if they are scientifically literate. Benchmarks coordinates with the work of Science for All Americans.
- *Atlas of Science Literacy Volume* 1 (2001) and *Atlas of Science Literacy Volume 2* (2007) use the benchmarks to map the clusters and the relationships among clusters across grade levels. This allows viewers to see the connections within and between grade-level bands as well as the prerequisites for a given idea or standard. This unique tool is useful in designing curriculum and instruction because it maps the interconnections of ideas of a scientifically literate person.
- *Designs for Science Literacy* (2001) explains how to use the three tools mentioned above with curriculum development processes. The processes explained in Designs are summarized here. This summary is one of the few in-depth discussions of how to use standards and standards-based tools to develop an aligned curriculum.

The National Research Council also wrote a set of standards for science, called *National Science Education Standards: Observe, Interact, Change, Learn* (1996). We'll look at the AAAS standards, however, because they discuss and focus on curriculum development and alignment.

AAAS PROJECT 2061—PURPOSE AND APPROACH

First, let's examine the three tools in the tool kit. Although science is the content area and it has close connections to mathematics, technology, and the social sciences, the processes could be used with any subject area, because most of these tools exist in national and state work on standards in other areas.

Science for All Americans (1989) defines what scientific literacy should be by the end of high school:

The desire for *science literacy for all citizens* led to the general goal that *all students* should be well educated in science, mathematics, and technology by the time they leave their common schooling. This in turn led to agreement on *five criteria* for identifying specific learning goals in science, mathematics, and technology: utility, social responsibility, intrinsic value of knowledge, philosophical value and childhood enrichment. Based on these criteria, *Science for All Americans* recommends 65 *major learning goals* to be reached by all students by the time they graduate from high school. (*Science for All Americans*, p. 50)

Figure 6.1 shows the titles of the sixty-five major learning goals. These learning goals can also be thought of as K–12 standards for science education. Local teachers and administrators will find this a useful tool as *Science for All Americans* (1989) provides the big picture of where science education should aim. Later we will describe how this tool can be used as part of staff development in curriculum planning. The drawback of this document is that it doesn't specify at what grade levels topics should be taught. *Benchmarks for Science Literacy* fills this gap.

Benchmarks for Science Literacy (1993) sequenced the K–12 goals for science literacy with benchmarks as the instructional focus of a range of grade levels (K–2, 3–5, 6–8, and 9–12). So, in Figure 6.1, topics are sequenced within a section; the topic "uncertainty" has eleven goals that are characteristic of a scientifically literate person beginning with understanding the topic "sources of uncertainty." The next column above shows how the benchmarks sequence the topics through grade-level bands of K–2, 3–5, 6–8, and 9–12. Local curriculum developers can use the benchmarks to help develop a scope and sequence for their science curriculum. For example, all of the K–2 benchmarks could be divided into those appropriate for each grade level. Then the local curriculum developers could develop units and activities to address each of the benchmarks. Later, we will see how the benchmarks can be used to eliminate unnecessary topics and vocabulary.

The *Atlas of Science Literacy* (2001, 2007) shows the relationship of the benchmarks to each other and to other topic areas through strand maps. Figure 6.2 is a strand map of gravity. Benchmarks have boxes around the learning goal with their benchmark code included. On the left-hand side are the grade-level bands for the benchmarks. The arrows between learning goal boxes "indicate that understanding one idea contributes to understanding the other, either logically or psychologically" (*Designs for Science Literacy*, 2001, p. 184) At the bottom of the chart are other topics or "story lines" that relate to an understanding of gravity

Figure 6.1   Organization of *Science for All Americans* and *Benchmarks for Science Literacy*

Organization of *Science for all Americans* and *Benchmarks for Science Literacy*

Within Domains of Science, Mathematics, and Technology

Chapter 1
The Nature of Science
The Scientific World View
The Scientific Enterprise

Chapter 2
The Nature of Mathematics
Patterns and Relationship
Mathematics, Science, and
  Technology
Mathematical Inquiry

Chapter 3
The Nature of Technology
Technology and Science
Design and Systems
Issues in Technology

Chapter 4
The Physical Setting
The Universe
The Earth
Processes That Shape the
  Earth
Structure of Matter
Energy Transformations
Motion
Forces of Nature

Chapter 5
The Living Environment
Diversity of Life
Heredity
Cells
Interdependence of Life
Flow of Matter and Energy
Evolution of Life

Chapter 6
The Human Organism
Human Identity
Human Development
Basic Functions
Learning
Physical Health
Mental Health

Chapter 7
Human Society
Cultural Effects on Behavior
Group Behavior
Social Change
Social Trade-Offs
Political and Economic
  Systems
Social Conflict
Global Interdependence

Chapter 8
The Designed World
Agriculture
Materials and Manufacturing
Energy Sources and Use
Communication
Information Processing
Health Technology

Chapter 9
The Mathematical World
Numbers
Symbolic Relationships
Shapes
Uncertainty
Reasoning

Chapter 10
Historical Perspectives
Displacing the Earth from the
  Center of the Universe
Uniting the Heavens and Earth
Relating Matter and Energy
  and Time and Space
Extending Time
Moving the Continents
Understanding Fire
Splitting the Atom
Explaining the Diversity of Life
Discovering Germs
Harnessing Power

Chapter 11
Common Themes
Systems
Models
Constancy and Change
Scale

Chapter 12
Habits of Mind
Values and Attitudes
Computation and Estimation
Manipulation and Observation
Communication Skills
Critical Response Skills

TOPIC/SEQUENCE WITHIN A SECTION

source of uncertainty

probability

estimating probability from
  data or theory

counts versus proportions

plots and alternative averages

importance of variation and
  around average

comparisons of proportions

correlation versus causation

learning about a whole from
  a part

common sources of bias

importance of sample size

BENCHMARKS

K–2
Often a person can find out
about a group of things by
studying just a few of them.

3–5
A small part of something may
be special in some way and not
give an accurate picture of the
whole. How much a portion of
something can help to estimate
what the whole is like depends
on how the portion is chosen.

6–8
The larger a well-chosen sample
is, the more accurately it is likely
to represent the whole. But
there are many ways of choosing
a sample that can make it
unrepresentative of the whole.

9–12
For a well chosen sample, the
size of the sample is much more
important than the size of the
population. To avoid intentional
or unintentional bias, samples
are usually selected by some
random system.

The learning goals in *Science for All Americans* and *Benchmark for Science Literacy* share the same organizational structure beginning
with the three broad domains of science, mathematics, and technology. Within these domains learning goals are distributed among 12
chapters, 65 sections within chapters, 250 topics within sections, and finally among more than 800 detailed benchmark statements within topics.

(i.e. changing motion, relative motion, and orbits.) Local curriculum developers can use the atlas and the strand maps to refine a scope and sequence. For example, the two benchmarks about Earth's gravity and changing motion at grades K–2 will need to be covered before the topics at Grades 3–5 can be introduced successfully to ensure that students have the appropriate prerequisite skills. (Remember Bloom's theory?) The maps will also help local curriculum developers understand the interrelationships among topics, such as the interrelationships between Earth's gravity and changing motion or relative motion. The maps do not specify one way or a best way to cover the topics, but they do tell local curriculum developers which major ideas students need to understand before tackling other ideas.

The alignment matrix in Figure 6.3 shows the areas addressed by AAAS's materials and processes.

Figure 6.2   Project 2061 Strand Map

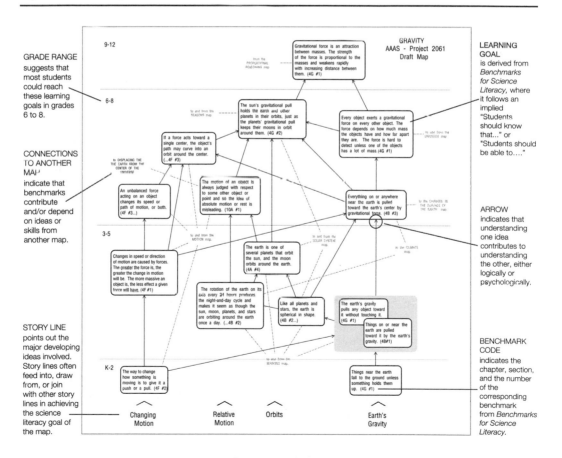

Figure 6.3   The Alignment Matrix—Project 2061

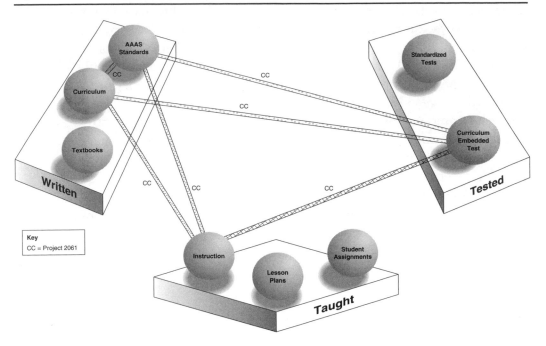

The alignment matrix reveals that Project 2061 was interested in the alignments between curriculum, curriculum-embedded tests, standards, and instruction. While the subjects are limited to mathematics and science, and while the authors offer no research validation for their recommendations, Project 2061 has been included in this book because of its systematic discussion of what districts can do to align their curriculum for improving achievement.

SUMMARY OF FINDINGS FOR PROJECT 2061

Alignment is one avenue by which to approach curriculum development. Curriculum alignment is only possible if a curriculum has been created. This chapter demonstrates that alignment can be a useful tool when embedded into a curriculum development process. In the next chapter we summarize the research by Schmidt et al. (2001) around a portion of the TIMMS that shows how curriculum affects achievement. The beginning of Part III describes one way of developing curriculum that recognizes the importance of aligning curriculum, standards, and assessments to curriculum and staff development processes that has produced dramatically improved results where development and implementation have been ensured. But first, here are some suggestions of how to use alignment to foster good curriculum development.

WHAT DISTRICTS CAN DO

AAAS outlines four areas where school districts can build professional capability for undertaking curriculum change:

1. How teachers acquire knowledge and skills regarding science itself

2. How science is represented in literacy goals or the standards

3. How students learn challenging ideas

4. How materials for instruction and assessment serve students' learning (*Designs for Science Literacy*, 2001, p 179)

AAAS has published a CD-ROM entitled *Resources for Science Literacy: Professional Development* which provides workshop outlines, lists of science trade books that address the content of *Science for All Americans* (1989), and summaries of cognitive research on how students learn challenging science ideas. This tool can help "teachers to acquire knowledge and skills regarding science itself."

#6–1

Clarify benchmarks.

Just having standards (what students should know and be able to do), such as *Science for All Americans* (1989) and *Benchmarks for Science Literacy* (1993), means that what is most important for students to learn has already been decided. States have used these national standards to inform the development of state standards. One staff development activity would be to compare the *Benchmarks for Science Literacy* to state standards for science, understanding that each state and national standards document has its own unique point of view. Understanding the similarities and differences among the documents is important. Having teachers clarify benchmarks (standards) is the first step in understanding how the pieces fit into the whole of science literacy. The five activities suggested in Figure 6.4 are listed in no particular order.

Figure 6.4 Using Project 2061 Tools to Clarify a Benchmark

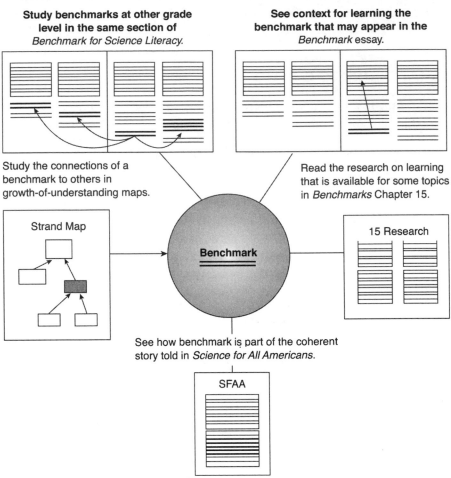

#6–2

Unburden the curriculum.

The goal of a national standards document, such as *Science for All Americans*, is twofold:

- To specify what students should know and be able to do
- To leave out content and ideas of lesser importance

This helps to reduce "excessive inclusiveness" with long lists of topics and vocabulary that need to be addressed in instruction. For example, a topic such as cells can imply a huge number of concepts and vocabulary. The *Benchmarks of Science Literacy* (1993) state:

Information transfer and energy transformation are functions of nearly all cells. The molecular aspects of these processes should wait until students have observed the transformation of energy in a variety of physical systems and have examined more generally the requirements for the transfer of information. (p. 110)

So, the *Benchmarks* make the following recommendation for teaching about cells for Grades 9–12:

The idea that protein molecules assembled by cells conduct the work that goes on inside and outside the cells in an organism can be learned without going into the biochemical details. (p. 112)

Biology and life science teachers at the high-school level then will want to examine their courses to determine if they are teaching more than is necessary according to the *Benchmarks*. If they are, they may want to reduce the depth of coverage so that other topic areas can be addressed and the connections between areas can be strengthened. Standards do provide what should be covered, but they also hold the key to understanding and reducing the scope of the curriculum, which according to the TIMMS is "a mile wide and an inch deep." Of course, this applies to not only science but to other subject areas and standards as well. Teachers will want to clarify how individual benchmarks (standards) fit into the whole, clarifying what is necessary and what makes the instruction too detailed.

#6–3

Cut major topics.

Figure 6.5 shows an analysis of the ideas included in traditional textbook series and the number of ideas that are omitted in the *Benchmarks*, as they were deemed not essential to producing scientifically literate students.

Figure 6.5   Benchmark Ideas Included in Traditional Science Curriculum

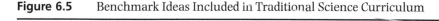

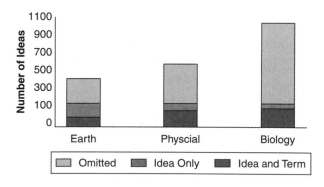

A typical biology textbook covers nearly 1,100 ideas and a typical school year is 180 days long. Covering all the ideas in a biology textbook would require a teacher to cover more than five ideas a day for 180 days, an impossible requirement. Unburdening the curriculum is necessary, and the *Benchmarks* assist teachers in pruning the curriculum. The following is a suggested procedure for teacher groups to develop a consensus on the topics needing elimination from the curriculum.

1. Discuss the distinction between (1) "topics" as categories of goals for what students will end up knowing or being able to do, and (2) "topics" as contexts for learning, rather than content to be learned. (They could consider just not using the word "topic" for one or the other of those meanings, but the word is so firmly embedded in education discourse that it is best to wrestle with it for a while.)

2. Begin with a list of topics in the current curriculum (often textbooks can serve as proxies for the curriculum) and indicate whether there are learning goals in *Benchmarks* that match. The various teams in the district can share and compare lists.

3. As the number of items on the lists grows, begin to make a master list of topics to be considered for elimination from the core. The criteria for making such judgments would, of course, have to take into account any pertinent district or state requirements.

4. From the list of candidate topics for elimination, each team member selects one topic to drop and identifies a core topic in which to invest the additional time made available.

5. Each team member evaluates the effect of dropping one topic and spending more time on another. It may be useful to consult with teachers in later grades about their expectations for what their students should already have learned. (Since those teachers too are struggling with the importance of topics, their advice is desirable but not definitive.) In each instance, after full discussion, the faculty team decides whether to recommend that other teachers in the district also drop the topic in question from the basic science and mathematics core. (*Designs for Science Literacy*, 2001, p. 217)

Figure 6.6   Traditional Topics to Consider Excluding From Literacy Core

Below are sample topic headings taken from typical textbooks under which few (if any) relevant benchmarks could be identified . . .		
from a typical **Physical Science** textbook		
Gas Laws	Flight	Electric Circuits
Periodic Table	Work and Power	Optics
Properties of Solutions	Simple Machines	Nuclear Reactors
Acids and Bases	Calorimetry	Mining
Nuclear Chemistry	Heating Systems	Petroleum Processing
	Engines	Electronics
		Computer Hardware
from a typical **Earth Science** textbook		
Solar Features	Lunar Features	Rivers
Stellar Evolution	Atmospheric Layers	Geological Eras
from a typical **Biology** textbook		
Branches of Biology		
Classification System		
from typical **Algebra** and **Geometry** textbooks		
Rational Expressions	Fractional Equations	Axiomatic Systems
Conic Sections	Quadratic Inequalities	Locus
Matrix Operations	Systems of Inequalities	Synthetic Methods
Polynomials		Right Triangle Trigonometry
Factoring		Sets and Truth Tables
Radical Expressions		

This process could be accomplished in other subject areas. Figure 6.6 lists some traditional topics to consider excluding from the curriculum.

Designs for Science Literacy also contains numerous lists of subtopics in algebra, geometry, biology, earth science, and physical science to consider for pruning.

#6–4

Trim technical vocabulary.

Yager (1983) reported vocabulary loads ranging from 2,173 words for a physical science textbook to over 17,130 words for a biology textbook. Groves (1995) followed-up this study, confirming that "the amount of vocabulary load presented is still too high and may contribute to the problem of science avoidance by secondary students" (p. 213) while finding less of a vocabulary load using a revised procedure. Such research suggests a need to systematically reduce vocabulary load.

Designs for Science Literacy suggests the following process:

Faculty teams can be set up to look for topics that seem to be overburdened with technical language and recommend which terms can reasonably be avoided. As suggested in the box on the opposite page, a list of topics can be considered to include three categories:

1. the concept and the technical term for the concept are both recommended for basic science literacy;

2. the concept is recommended, but not the technical term;

3. neither the concept nor technical term is recommended. As the faculty teams study the terminology associated with a topic, they can question the judgment expressed in the list and modify it if they wish, but only after discussion and then only if persuasive arguments for including the technical terms are made.

The burden is on having to show why technical words that go beyond what is needed for science literacy should be included, not on having to argue for their exclusion. (p. 133)

#6–5

Reduce wasteful repetition.
When developing or revising a curriculum, teachers will want to eliminate unnecessary repetition of topics and concepts, while understanding that some repetition is beneficial.

1. Cross-grade teacher teams should conduct an informal survey to see which topics appear to be frequently repeated in the K–12 curriculum.

2. Choosing from the resulting list of topics likely to have excess redundancy, the teams should analyze one for which a growth-of-understanding map exists. By comparing entries on the map to the profile of the topic given in the district curriculum, the team can locate differences.

3. By studying these differences, the team can think through just what component ideas may be learned and when, with

what level of understanding, and with what means to demonstrate that understanding.

Note that this recommendation is for a collaborative investigation of what it takes for students to learn, not for high-school teachers to instruct middle-school teachers, nor for middle-school teacher to instruct elementary-school teachers, in what they should accomplish with students. (*Designs for Science Literacy*, 2001, pp. 234–235)

#6–6

Learn to analyze curriculum materials.

Once the benchmarks are clarified and teachers understand them deeply, then teachers can turn to an analysis of curriculum materials. The focus here is "Do the curriculum materials actually help students to achieve the benchmarks in a powerful way?" (*Designs for Science Literacy*, 2001, p. 193). This assumes that a curriculum has been developed that is aligned to the benchmarks or the state standards. If a curriculum has been developed, then curriculum materials can be analyzed and evaluated based on whether they help to meet the goals. Returning to our cell example, if the biology text presented the biochemical details of the protein molecules in the cells while giving little attention to the more general work that goes on within and without these cells, then new material will need to be found so that the curriculum material can be in balance with the stated aims of the curriculum. Too often, teachers assume that if topics are included in the textbook, they should be taught to students. Learning to analyze curriculum materials, such as textbooks, given the framework of the benchmarks or standards is important in the continuing effort to unburden the curriculum. (Chapter 3 provides more details about how to examine textbooks.)

#6–7

Align assessment to curriculum.

After developing a curriculum, the next step is to create assessments. To be fair, assessments need to be aligned with the goals and content of the curriculum. Teachers need to ask whether the assessment actually indicates whether a student individually, or students as a group, have mastered the goals and content of the curriculum.

In fact, assessment provides only sample performances of how a goal might be met, with the assessor making the inference that good performance on the assessment means that the student has mastered the complete goal, as shown in Figure 6.7.

Figure 6.7   Inferences Based on Assessments

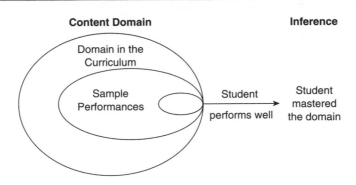

Teachers need to consider the alignment of the content domain with the domain covered within the curriculum. Then teachers need to wrestle with whether the sample performances adequately align to and represent the domain. Lastly, teachers need to decide whether the following inference is true: students have indeed adequately learned the content of the domain if they performed well on the sample performance. Underlying all this is the question, What does "mastery" mean at this stage of a student's development? Documents like *Science for All Americans* and *Benchmarks* can help to specify the domains so that sample performances can be appropriately developed. Other standards from other subject areas can perform a similar function.

Alignment of assessment also needs to address how data from the assessment are used to monitor curriculum. Districts need to build assessment systems that

1. Assess individual students;

2. Aggregate assessments so that teachers will have data with which to make an inference about whether students have learned the curriculum;

3. Aggregate the assessment data so that district and school strengths and needs in delivery of the curriculum across teachers can be gathered;

4. Provide a procedure for linking the data and the results to a staff development and curriculum development plan for the district and a school improvement plan for the schools.

#6–8

Relate instructional units to strand maps.

The strand maps from the *Atlas of Science Literacy* (2001) provide a way for aligning units of instruction to the *Benchmarks* to ensure adequate

Figure 6.8   Relating Instructional Units to Strand Maps

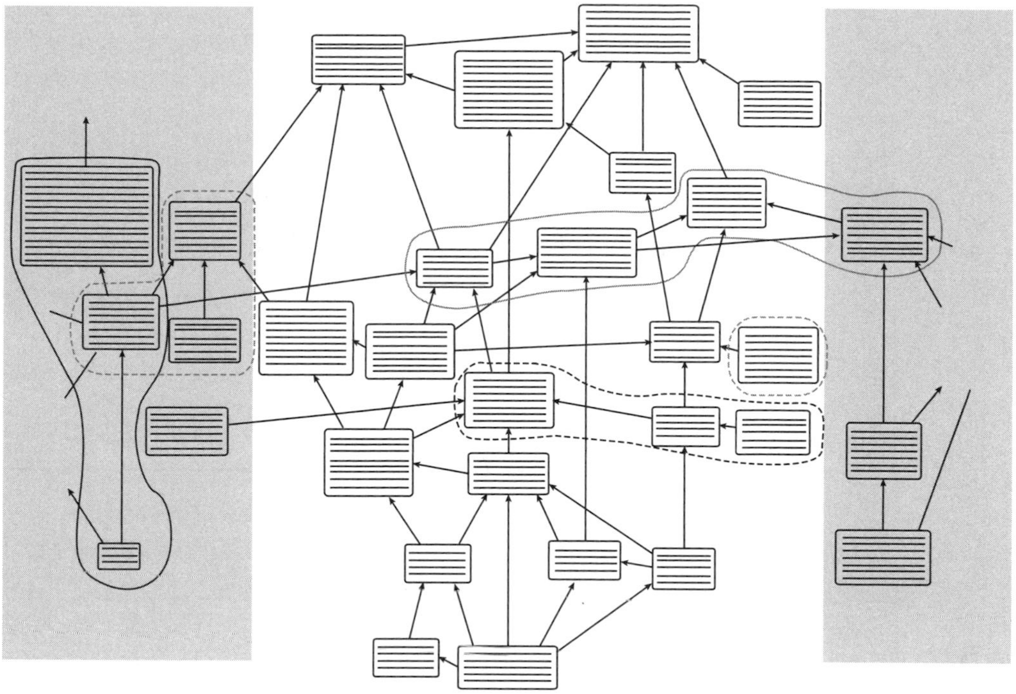

| Instructional Units | The Lives of Plants | Food, Energy, and Growth | Matter and Molecules | Chemistry That Applies |

This diagram—derived from a composite of several maps from *Atlas of Science Literacy*—Illustrates how instructional units can be related to strand maps. Loops on the maps enclose the benchmarks served by each unit. The *Matter and Molecules* unit serves a generally 'vertical' set of learning goals, addressing a sequence of ideas over time. On the other hand, the *Lives of Plants* unit and the *Food, Energy, and Growth* unit serve a mostly "horizontal" set of goals, addressing a variety of ideas at approximately the same grade level. More than one unit can address the same idea, often a benefit if it is a particularly difficult idea

coverage in instruction. They also describe the most important aspects of units. The diagram in Figure 6.8 shows how units might be related to the strand map. Loops on the map indicates major areas covered by units of instruction.

#6–9

Create strand maps for other subject areas.

The Atlas of Science Literacy (2001) demonstrates the usefulness of strand maps. Given that all standards help to create a picture of an integrated whole for a given subject area, constructing strand maps using standards in other subject areas is possible. Creating strand maps involves four steps:

1. Develop grade-level bands.

2. Map strands (major themes of the subject area). Put strands [themes] with the most connections next to each other.

3. Organize standards within strands, mapping their connections and demonstrating their prerequisites.

4. Chart major connections between noncontiguous strands.

Each step is described further below.

Start with a big sheet of paper, such as paper used for flip charts.

1. *Develop grade-level bands.* Put the grade-level bands covered by the standards on the left-hand side. Indicate the top level of each band by placing a demarcation line, as in the Figure 6.9.

Figure 6.9   Sample Strand Configuration

2. *Map strands.* Most standards are divided into themes, or major areas in that subject matter, that should be aligned to curriculum. For example, the Michigan Framework for Social Studies is divided into the following strands:

- Historical Perspective
- Geographic Perspective
- Civic Perspective
- Economic Perspective

- Inquiry
- Public Discourse and Decision Making
- Citizen Involvement

These strands would be placed along the top of the sheet.

Figure 6.10   Standard Strands Mapped Across Grade Levels

Historical	Geographic	Civic	Economic	Inquiry	Public Discourse	Involvement
9–12						
6–8						
3–5						
K–2						

Further subdivisions are possible along the top, for example, the strand "Historical Perspective" is divided into numerous subthemes that could also be placed across the top of the paper. Or you could create a multipage map by placing three or four subthemes on a separate page.

3. *Organize standards within strands.* The standards for each of the strands are then placed in the appropriate grade-level band. Those that are most basic are placed in the lower levels of the grade-level band. Those that have prerequisites are placed higher. Then the standards within the strands are connected with arrows and lines. The direction of the arrows is always over or up. Arrows "indicate that understanding one idea contributes to understanding the other, either logically of psychologically" (*Designs for Science Literacy*, 2001, p. 184). Figure 6.11 is a strand map highlighting the strand "Earth's gravity" organized across grade-level bands.

Figure 6.11 Strand Map of Earth's Gravity Organized Across Grade Levels

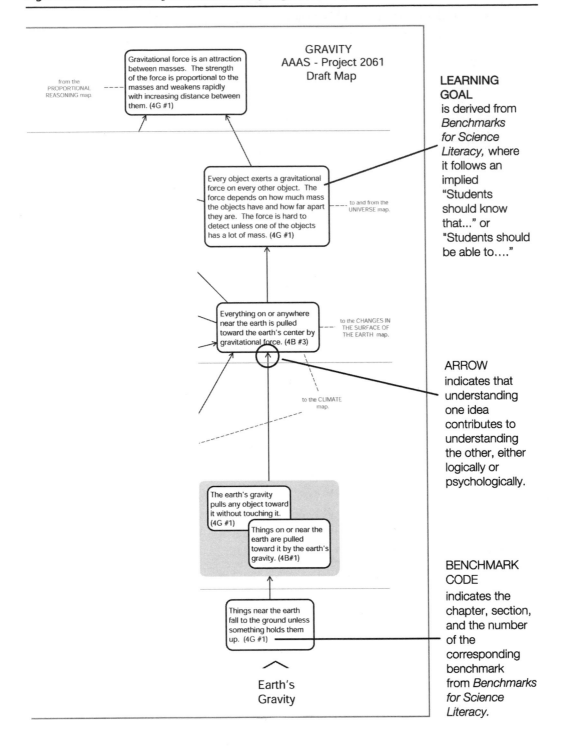

Figure 6.12   Chart Major Connections Between Noncontiguous Strands

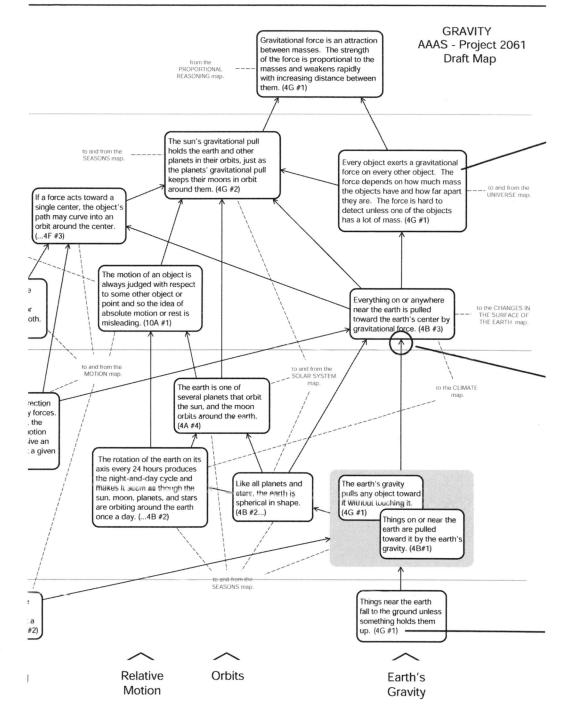

4.   Chart major connections between noncontiguous strands.

Note the strands next to "Earth's gravity" are "orbits" and "moon." Arrows are drawn to indicate that understanding one idea helps with the understanding of the other. Be parsimonious in showing relationships between standards, always indicating only the most important.

If strand maps are completed before curriculum development begins, the activity will promote an understanding of the standards, the relationship of the standards to each other, and the interconnections of the strands, or themes, with other strands or themes in the subject area. It will also help to generate consensus among the curriculum authors about what the curriculum needs to focus on and some alternative ways to construct the units that make up the curriculum.

Curriculum Makes
a Difference—
Alignment and the
TIMSS Analysis

T his chapter concentrates on part of the Third International Mathematics and Science Study (TIMSS). We single out this study because it suggests that curriculum is the most important variable in predicting student performance between countries. This means that curriculum is more important than socioeconomic status in producing results. That confirms other smaller studies that have similar findings (see Chapter 4 on mastery learning, for example). I have chosen to concentrate on this study because of its scope and the rigor of its analysis.

This mammoth study of students in over forty countries teased out some of the variables that affected performance in math and science. If students in Japan and Thailand perform better in mathematics than those in the United States, what helps to produce those differences? The study generated many books and articles, like Howson's work (1995) already cited in Chapter 3. Schmidt et al. (2001) in their book *Why Schools Matter: A Cross-National Comparison of Curriculum and Learning* show that the content of a country's curriculum affects student achievement in that country. TIMSS is the largest and most rigorous study of curriculum (and alignment) yet produced, and the results are stunning.

Those are the headlines. How did TIMSS reach the conclusion that curriculum affects student achievement? To answer this question, let's unpack the study's methodology.

THE TIMSS METHODOLOGY—PURPOSE AND APPROACH

Japan does better than the United States on producing math outcomes, but the United States has a different culture than Japan. There are different numbers of school days, books, directions on how to use the curriculum, and tests. How can we make a valid and reliable conclusion that Japan is better than the United States in producing math outcomes? Isn't this comparing apples and oranges?

These are the challenges for researchers in cross-national studies. Understanding how they designed the study helps us to also understand how they confronted these challenges in order to draw valuable conclusions about national performance.

The TIMSS Frameworks

The first problem the researchers confronted was how to describe what happens in classrooms, what is contained in textbooks, and what is tested. They needed a standard way to describe content so that the content could be compared across countries. If one textbook contains ten pages about ratio, and a textbook from another country barely mentions ratio, that may make a difference in the outcome for ratio. To solve this problem, the researchers developed the TIMSS Framework Topics for both mathematics and science. (These resemble state standards in mathematics and science.) For example, the following (see Figure 7.1) are three categories for fraction and decimals from the TIMSS Mathematics Framework:

Figure 7.1   Three Categories From the TIMSS Mathematics Framework

1.1.2 Fractions and Decimals

    1.1.2.1 Common Fractions

    1.1.2.2. Decimal Fractions

    1.1.2.3 Relationships of Common and Decimal Fractions

    1.1.2.4 Percentages

    1.1.2.5 Properties of Common and Decimal Fractions

SOURCE: From Schmidt et al., 2001, p. 364.

There were ten large categories for mathematics content (fractions and decimals being part of the major area of numbers) and eight large categories in science. Each contained subcategories so that the universe of curriculum topics in math and science were adequately described. Two other dimensions, performance expectations and general perspectives, filled out the universe of possibilities. Under performance expectations, or how a student is expected to demonstrate knowledge, there were five categories: knowing, using routine procedures, investigating and problem solving, mathematical reasoning, and communicating. There were five categories under general perspectives: attitudes, careers, participation by underrepresented groups, interest, and habits of mind.

The TIMSS frameworks provided a standard way to describe the content for instruction, for textbooks, and for the TIMSS tests. It also provided a way to sample teachers' lesson plans. The content of the plans could be coded using the TIMSS frameworks, therefore it would not matter which country you were coding. The results could be compared across countries because the TIMSS frameworks were identical for each country.

The TIMSS frameworks established the base for developing teacher questionnaires and student tests that were the same for all the countries in the study, thus ensuring that teacher actions revealed in the surveys and student results could be compared across countries. In other words, the TIMSS frameworks ensured alignment in the data collected across countries.

The TIMSS researchers collected four data sources on curriculum:

- Content standards coded to the TIMSS frameworks
- Textbook space coded to the TIMSS frameworks
- Teacher content goals (from teacher questionnaires) coded to the TIMSS frameworks
- Duration of content coverage (from teacher logs) coded to the TIMSS frameworks

Again, these data could be compared because they were coded based on the TIMSS frameworks. The methodology is described further in Webb (1997). More complete documentation is available in Robitaille et al. (1993) and Schmidt et al. (2001).

Selection of Students

Two samples of students gathered from three sets of adjacent grade levels were used in the study for example, majority nine-year-olds (i.e., third- and fourth-grade students), majority thirteen-years-old (seventh- and eighth-grade students), and eleventh- and twelfth-grade students ending up in their last year of schooling who are still studying math and science. Because both third and fourth graders were included in the study of nine-year-olds, this study, instead of looking at nine-year-olds as one group, divided them into two groups: those in third grade and those in fourth grade. Looking at the textbook space for topics, teacher goals, and duration of content coverage and comparing these to the TIMSS test scores, it is possible to note how students improved their achievement from, for example, the seventh to the eighth grade. (This is not a true longitudinal study because the samples were gathered at the same time using different cohorts of students.)

TIMSS Tests

The TIMSS tests in math and science were designed to assess the content of the TIMSS frameworks. TIMSS tests in math and science were given to the nine-year-old, thirteen-year-old, and secondary students. The results of these tests provided the outcome data for this study. As the tests were administered across nations at adjacent grade levels, the results between nations were compared and gains computed. The researchers could then delve into the four curriculum variables to determine which ones were associated with differences in test score gains.

Scope of the TIMSS

In the TIMSS analysis, instead of looking at the relationship of one aspect of alignment to another (e.g., textbook to test alignment), the researchers simultaneously examined a number of variables and found that curriculum (defined as country standards and textbooks) influenced instruction (defined as teacher goals and time teachers spend on content topics). In turn, that influenced achievement on TIMSS tests.

The results of the TIMSS is that elaborate comparisons could be made between countries: their curriculum, their textbooks, and their outcomes (a test developed by TIMSS researchers). For example, in the United States TIMSS characterized math instruction as a "mile wide and an inch deep" because the curriculum covered more topics than most other countries, and consequently, teachers had less time to spend on each of the topics. This coverage pattern was reinforced by textbooks and state department of education curriculum guides (Webb, 1997).

FINDINGS—SCHMIDT ET AL. LINK CURRICULUM AND STUDENT ACHIEVEMENT

Schmidt et al. (2001) examined the TIMSS data to see if there was a relationship between the curriculum, instruction, and student achievement.

The data consisted of indicators of curriculum (subject area content standards and textbook analysis), instruction (percent of topics covered and instructional time defined as the amount of time on topics), and the TIMSS test (which measured achievement growth resulting from a year of instruction). Schmidt et al. hypothesized and found that curriculum (what is covered) influences student achievement.

To demonstrate that curriculum influences achievement, the researchers proposed to test the following models (see Figure 7.2).

Figure 7.2 Structural Model Relating Curriculum and Achievement

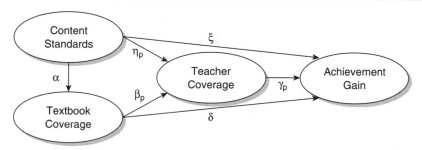

(a) Percent of Teachers in a Country (p) Teaching the Topic

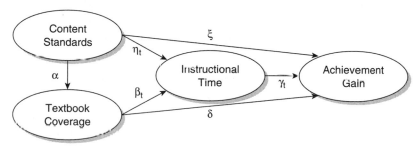

(b) Percent of the Instructional Time (t) Spent by a Teacher on the Topic Averaged over Teachers in a Country

These models show the interrelationships between content standards, textbook coverage, teacher coverage, instructional time, and achievement gains.

The first model emphasizes teacher coverage of content and its relationship to achievement gains. The second model emphasizes the relationship of instructional time to achievement gains. Here content standards influence textbook coverage; textbook coverage influences instructional time and achievement gains. Remember that Schmidt et al. (2001) are using the term *curriculum* to mean content standards and textbook coverage; and *instruction* to mean teacher coverage or instructional time. Both models show that content standards and textbook coverage (the two circles on the far left side of the diagram) affect teacher coverage and instructional time, as well as influence achievement gains. The authors examined only mathematics in the middle school years, not science. How did the model hold up when Schmidt and his colleagues looked at the actual TIMSS data?

Results show there was a relationship between these variables (content standards, textbook coverage, teacher coverage, and instructional time) and achievement gains in the subject area.

> Statistically significant relationships existed between each of the curriculum aspects and learning as characterized by estimated achievement gains from seventh to eighth grade. . . . The more curriculum coverage of a topic area—no matter whether manifested as emphasis in content standard, as proportion of textbook space, or as measured by either teacher implementation variable (coverage or instructional time)—is related to larger gains in that same topic area. (Schmidt et al., 2001, p. 261)

Stated another way: "The curricular priorities of a country—whether reflected by content standards, textbooks, or teacher behavior—are related to the profile of achievement gains across topics for that country" (Schmidt et al., 2001, p. 261). Note that the level of analysis is by country, and of course it varies for different countries, but the general relationship still holds.

"For both mathematics and science, the direct relationship between textbook coverage and learning was defined at the topic level" (Schmidt et al., 2001, p. 267). This means that the amount of coverage of topics in the textbook determined how well students did on the TIMSS test. If there were many pages of coverage for perimeter, area, and volume, then students' results on the items for perimeter, area, and volume were higher than in countries with fewer pages in the textbook. The study also found a relationship between time spent on the topic across countries. "Higher percentages of coverage on a typical topic that involved more demanding performance expectations were associated with larger-than-average achievement gains" (Schmidt et al., 2001, p. 303). This supports previous recommendations for the United States to cover fewer topics in math and science while devoting more time to each topic.

We see how curriculum is associated with achievement. In other international studies of achievement, researchers only reported how students did, not how much they gained. Those achievement statistics (how well students did) significantly correlated with measures of the countries' wealth or economic development. Would the same correlation between wealth and achievement gains hold true during the year of the TIMSS for students at contiguous grade levels? (Remember, in the chapter on mastery learning, Wishnick (1986) had found that an aligned curriculum reduced the influence of socioeconomic status on student achievement to almost zero. Similar results were found by Price-Baugh (1997) and Moss-Mitchell (1998).)

The study found that GNP (gross national product) as a measure of a country's wealth was not strongly related to achievement gains in either math or science (in science only three topics out of seventeen had significant relationships) [Schmidt et al., 2001, p. 319]. This confirms the findings of Wishnick and Price-Baugh, reported earlier, that discovered little relationship between socioeconomic status and student outcome when alignment was controlled. The finding also suggests that the content of curriculum and instruction are more important than socioeconomic status in determining learning gains.

The study went deeper into the data, looking at achievement just in the United States and controlled for socioeconomic status and prior achievement in mathematics (science wasn't analyzed in this way). "The general conclusion is that curriculum or OTL (Opportunity to Learn) was significantly related to achievement in U.S. eighth-grade math classrooms" (Schmidt et al., 2001, p. 340). Explained another way: ". . .differences in learning among U.S. eighth-grade mathematics classrooms were related to concomitant differences in the amount of instructional time that teachers allocated to supporting curriculum areas even when we adjusted for differences among classrooms due to SES [socioeconomic status] and prior learning. This was true in all subtest areas (except two)" [Schmidt et al., 2001, pp. 341–342].

For student learning, the extent of opportunities to learn curriculum content matters. The more time a teacher spends on a topic, the greater achievement score for that topic. Effect sizes, as measured by R^2, were between .4 and .6 thereby explaining a significant portion of the variance.

In other words, on average, for a classroom that spent about one week more on a topic than another classroom, where the two classrooms were similar in SES [socioeconomic status] composition and in terms of prior achievement, the former would have a predicted achievement score some 3 to 24 percentage points higher than that of the other class. Thus, it seems unsurprising that even a small amount of additional instruction (as little as a week for each) focused on these key topics would predict large increases in learning (around 20 percentile points). (Schmidt et al., 2001, p. 344)

The big idea is that a significant relationship exists between achievement gains and curriculum. "Schools matter because through the curriculum they provide a systematic opportunity for students to learn and master the subject matter contents and processes necessary for their successful living. . . . Curriculum mattered to learning in mathematics and the sciences. In case after case, some significant relationship was found between achievement gains and curriculum" (Schmidt et al., 2001, p. 355). Curriculum is something that school districts control, even with the existence of state standards and state tests. Although the study points out the influences of standards and textbooks on curriculum decisions by teachers, right now most school personnel are not familiar with curriculum structures that will have an effect on student achievement (for more on this see Chapters 8 and 9).

Figure 7.3   The Alignment Matrix—The TIMSS

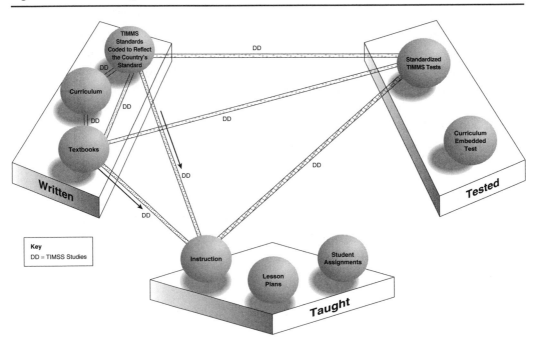

The alignment matrix in Figure 7.3 shows the complex alignment relationships demonstrated in the TIMSS. Note that the two lines have directional arrows, which means that textbooks and standards have a demonstrated influence on the content of instruction.

WHAT DISTRICTS CAN DO

It is of paramount importance to make sure students have the opportunity to learn important content aligned with standards and assessments. Curriculum for school districts is no longer "just nice to have." Curriculum is a necessity for furthering student achievement. Further, school districts, through their curricula, have the tools at their disposal to control and ensure what students learn. We need a surge of district led curriculum writing aligned with important content area standards to ensure that all children will learn. These studies indicate that achievement gains will follow.

#7–1

Decide on fewer topics covered in more depth, particularly in math.

Many mathematics textbooks, in order to be all things to all school districts and cover all topics listed in all state standards, cover too many topics. Students don't get the depth they need because they cover many topics in a cursory manner. The TIMSS showed that countries that cover fewer topics per year generally have higher achievement. This suggests that districts need to reduce the number of topics covered so more depth is possible.

Districts can set up pacing charts keyed to textbooks and other instructional material that will give teachers guidance on what topics are most important to cover. The pacing guide can be developed by representative teachers from across the district. One difficulty with this approach is that there may not be enough material in the textbooks to ensure depth of coverage. Supplemental material or items available on the Internet are one way to solve this problem. Some districts share textbooks from the grade level above and below so there is enough material for the expanded time. Others have begun to place teacher made material on the district's Web site, and thus solve the distribution issue in that way.

Pluses

- Spending more time on fewer topics has been demonstrated to improve achievement on those topics.
- Teachers would be more sure about what to cover and the materials for covering the specified topics.

Other Considerations

- It may be difficult to gather enough teaching material for in-depth coverage of fewer topics.

- Textbooks may not contain enough material for in-depth coverage of fewer topics.
- Everybody else doesn't do it this way.

#7–2

Develop districtwide tests, aligned to state assessments, to gain data on students' mastery of topics.

Many districts have developed quarterly assessments that are in the same format as the state tests. Many of these tests, however, aren't aligned to the curriculum that was covered since the last test. Having such a test would allow districts to make data-based decisions about whether the students learned what they were taught.

Pluses

- Tests provide a standard way to determine effectiveness across teachers.
- If state tests don't report scores for topics, the district scores would be valuable for helping the district to improve its effectiveness.

Other Considerations

- The tests would need to be constructed such that they are reliable and valid, and many districts don't have that capacity.
- The tests need to be based on a curricular scope and sequence, and not every district has a curriculum that guides instruction in this way.
- Data from testing could be used in the teacher evaluation process.

#7–3

Use test results to vary time and coverage of key topics.

If state tests present their results by topic or by item, it is possible for districts to use this information to make changes in the amount of time spent on various topics. Representative teacher committees in various subject areas could do this when the results of the tests are returned to the district. For example, if students did well in a particular topic, then the district could consider reducing the amount of time spent on that topic. Conversely, if students didn't do well on a topic, then the district may want to consider spending more time on it. Districts that develop this approach need to ensure that principals monitor that teachers are spending the appropriate time and following the district's guidelines.

Pluses

- Time spent on topics is flexible rather than fixed and can be modified based on test data.

Other Considerations

- It may be difficult to monitor teachers' use of time across the district.
- Defining time for a topic area won't help if everyone doesn't have a good idea of what should be covered in the topic area.
- Defining what should be covered in a topic may necessitate some staff development activities if teachers don't have background in that particular topic area.

Part III

The Aligned Curriculum

Part II described three systematic ways to address alignment and showed how they could improve achievement. Part III poses criteria for systematically addressing alignment issues through curriculum. One curriculum model called the Balanced Curriculum, developed specifically to systematically address alignment issues, is described. We will see how it meets the criteria for addressing alignment issues. The book ends with a chapter showing how the Balanced Curriculum meets many of the book's recommendations for district interventions. The model has demonstrated that addressing alignment issues through curriculum improves student achievement, with a summary of results from districts who have implemented the model.

Criteria for a Useful and Usable Curriculum Incorporating Alignment

In previous chapters alignment issues were spelled out in detail through the various alignment categories on the alignment matrix. The research clearly shows that alignment is essential to improving student achievement. Many of the alignment strategies proposed in this book take pieces of the alignment puzzle and show how districts can address these specific areas.

Chapter 7 summarized research suggesting that an aligned curriculum is a major influence in producing student achievement. Thus, the focus of this chapter is on curriculum, not on alignment. We will examine how to structure a district's curriculum in order to harness alignment's power through a systematic curriculum development process. What would happen if curriculum structures systematically incorporated all the different aspects of alignment so the pieces worked together to create a powerful whole that improved student achievement? Then, if a district were to develop the curriculum using this structure, they could be assured that the many alignment issues suggested by the research are addressed, and student achievement would improve as a result of using an alignment-inclusive curriculum.

In this chapter, we will put together a rationale for structuring curriculum. It contrasts our definition of curriculum with a common definition of curriculum. The details of this chapter also demonstrate how our definition of curriculum works because it incorporates the research about alignment. The chapter ends with ten criteria for a useful and usable curriculum that will help districts determine whether their design capitalizes on the alignment research.

One systematic way to incorporate many of the individual suggestions made in this book is through curriculum design. After this chapter's discussion of elements of a curriculum definition, Chapter 9 will present the Balanced Curriculum as one systematic and research-based way to design curriculum that accounts for alignment and demonstrates achievement gains.

THE MANY MEANINGS OF CURRICULUM

Curriculum has many different meanings. The alignment matrix used throughout this book illustrates some of those meanings.

Figure 8.1   The Alignment Matrix

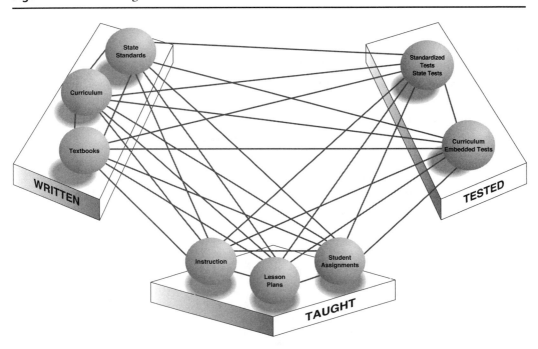

Some researchers emphasized that textbooks or state standards are the curriculum because they provide guidance on what students know and are able to do. Others believe that it is the instructional elements. The lesson plans or the student assignments represent the curriculum to other researchers, because these elements specify what students know and should be able to do on a daily basis. These various definitions present different levels of specificity (e.g., a lesson plan versus state standards). The definitions also take into account different time perspectives (daily for lesson planning versus yearly or longer for state standards). Only by knowing how curriculum is defined will we be able to ensure the continuous, positive achievement effects promised in the alignment research.

THE COMMON DEFINITION OF CURRICULUM

Let's begin with the common definition of curriculum to show the way school districts typically define curriculum: Curriculum sets the goals for instruction; teachers independently decide how to achieve those goals. For many educators, curriculum is just a list of goals agreed upon by the organization. The educators decide how to meet the goals by making decisions about time (i.e., how much time to spend on achieving the goal) and the process of how to go about teaching. The common definition reinforces the agreement between the organization and educator about goals for instruction. In this case, teachers have the autonomy to interpret the goals for instruction in any way. Districts specify the goals and individual teachers decide how to meet the goals in their classes, with little or no accountability (i.e., checking to see if the goals were addressed or accomplished) from district- or school-level administration. Many districts still operate in this manner today.

Enter the standards movement. Standards—what students should know and be able to do—set the goals for instruction. Operating within their authority, the state replaced the district in setting the goals. Districts now have to find a way to meet those goals. If the previous agreements are continued, then individual teachers have the authority to decide how and when to enact the standards. Little checking on whether the goals are taught or met occurs. Again, many school districts continue these arrangements.

Standards increase pressure on districts because achievement is assessed by high-stakes state tests with highly publicized results. These hold districts, superintendents, schools, and principals responsible for progress, or the lack thereof, and students' performance on standards-based state assessments. Additionally, No Child Left Behind legislation requires that all children be proficient on their state test by 2014. Many states and districts have a long way to go.

Curriculum's common agreement that districts (or states) propose the goals and that individual teachers decide how the goals will be realized needs to change in order to meet the current realities of the standards movement, accountability, and No Child Left Behind. It needs to change because teachers working individually have no way of aligning their instruction or their individual curriculum. To do so would be too inefficient and cost prohibitive. Yet, as the research points out, alignment is the key to unlocking improved student achievement.

Districts tend to address pieces of the alignment issue by implementing a few of the actions suggested in previous chapters of this book. For example, a district may reason that quarterly assessments will provide the necessary information to predict results on the yearly state assessment. This "test more" strategy assumes that the additional testing and feedback will help teachers make the right decisions about what to teach and how to teach it, thus scores on the quarterly assessments and yearly state test will improve.

Districts respond to pressure by enacting a combination of strategies that specify *when* content is taught, *what* content is taught, and *how* content is taught. For example, pacing guides may outline *when* topics are taught and *what* topics are taught, thus leaving it to the individual teacher's choice as to *how* topics are taught within the time constraints. The how-to-teach part of the alignment process is absent. Greater variability in teaching occurs if how to teach is not addressed. Test scores will reflect this variability.

To address this problem, some districts adopt prescriptive programs such as *Success for All—Roots and Wings for Elementary School Reading*, a script that tells teachers what to say and do (Slavin & Madden, 2003). Such programs address how-to-teach issues by scripting individual lessons for all teachers. Unfortunately, they do not address how well the program's content may be aligned to state standards and assessments. The program's generally positive results suggest that controlling for teacher variability when implementing curriculum can result in positive achievement gains. To maximize these gains, however, alignment with state standards and assessments must occur in order to capitalize on alignment's ability to produce higher student achievement.

The main flaw with curriculum is that of individual variation between teachers. Because individual teachers decide how and when to teach the standards (goals), no two teachers will produce the same results, and the risk for large variations in test scores between teachers increases significantly.

There is no way for individual teachers to align the instruction with the standards, except to hope that the teachers have read the hundreds of standards statements and integrated them when instructing their students. Such hope is futile because it is impossible for teachers to keep hundreds of standards statements in their heads while making thousands of decisions during instruction. If teachers individually decide what and how to teach, then there is little alignment between classroom instruction and state standardized tests. What alignment there is probably will vary tremendously among teachers. As a result, this virtually guarantees that alignment of curriculum and standards across the professional teaching community of the school district will not and cannot occur. Consequently, standardized test results will not improve.

Implementing the common definition of curriculum will not work. For a curriculum to capture the power of alignment, the curriculum needs to specify *when* the content is taught, *what* content is taught, and *how* the content is taught. Our definition of curriculum contains these elements.

OUR DEFINITION OF CURRICULUM

I call this definition of curriculum the standards-based definition and, in contrast with the common definition, this one states:

> Curriculum is the district's written plan incorporating aspects of time use, content, and process aligned to standards and assessments that establishes a focus for instruction, assessment, staff development, and management so student achievement improves.

Let's examine each phrase in the definition to understand its implications.

"Curriculum is the district's written plan . . ."

The district is the definition's focus because the district has the responsibility of determining how the standards are enacted, not the schools or individual teachers as occurs in the common definition. The focus emerges from a resource issue: Most schools and individual teachers do not have the time or resources to produce, maintain, and improve a written plan for instruction other than lesson plans.

" . . . incorporating aspects of time use, content, and process . . ."

A curriculum needs to demonstrate how time will be used (Walberg, 1988). Many districts already have pacing guides that specify how much time is used on particular topics or units; therefore, a curriculum needs to specify the content to be covered during a particular time period. Time management for teaching core concepts, therefore, becomes an integral part of the process for covering important curricular content. No longer can individual teachers make individual decisions about what and when to teach important content. But we will discuss more about this later.

Finally, the district stipulates the process by which important content is covered. For example, teaching main idea by asking students to develop newspaper headlines is a powerful teaching technique that specifies the process by which the concept main idea is taught. Linking content and process together in the standards-based curriculum is different from the common definition of curriculum where only content or goals are specified and the process is under the purview of the individual teacher. Under the common definition, main idea might be taught by using sample state test questions about main idea or any one of a hundred different instructional methods, increasing variability across the school and district. Experienced teachers can distinguish between powerful and weak ways to address content. Their expertise should be incorporated into the curriculum so the most powerful teaching strategies can be used on a systematic basis. If all of the curriculum's goals are addressed with powerful strategies that all students had access to, achievement would likely improve.

" . . . aligned to standards and assessments . . ."

Standards-based curricula require that time, content, and process be described and aligned to standards and assessments. The common definition does not even consider alignment to state standards. By demonstrating *in writing* how standards will be met, we fulfill a primary function of the education system. Curricula becomes evidence-based, as illustrated by all of the research cited in this book.

" . . . that establishes a focus for instruction, assessment, staff development and management . . ."

A link has already been established between curriculum and instruction, but curriculum is also connected to assessment, staff development processes, and management functions. These issues have traditionally not been part of curriculum design.

If curriculum is a written plan for instruction, it must be linked to the instruction that takes place in the classroom. By now, it should be clear that this link includes the instructional process, how the standards are actually delivered in the classroom, and specifies how time is used.

In addition, we must ask ourselves How well do students know? How ably can they perform? These are assessment questions that are not separate from curriculum but intimately related to it, as the *Understanding by Design* framework for curriculum development demonstrates (Wiggins & McTighe, 2005).

Curriculum structures also require management. Through management processes, the district knows that the curriculum (written plan) is assessed and then implemented. Decisions, based on good data, can then be made about whether to improve, maintain, or modify the written plan.

" . . . so student achievement improves."

Regardless of how student achievement is defined, curriculum should be aligned to assessments in order to demonstrate improvements or identify achievement declines. Improved achievement is the outcome of a well developed, aligned, and implemented curriculum. If student achievement is not improving, then districts need to reexamine their curriculum development plan.

If the function of the district's curriculum is not to improve achievement, then developing a curriculum is not productive work. If the written plan (the curriculum) did not work the first time, then changes need to be made so it will work better the second time. This book demonstrates that the key component of curriculum is alignment. Those changes to the written plan give the district the necessary data and tools to revise the curriculum. For example, if achievement decreased in the persuasive writing section of the state assessment, was it because of

- time or lack of time spent on persuasive essays?
- how persuasive essays were taught and learned?
- the alignment between instruction and standards and the way the standards are assessed?
- unit assessments that do not align with the standardized assessments?
- the management of the curriculum? Was the concept taught by teachers in the district? Were there early warnings from district or unit assessments that there were problems? Did this data come to decision makers in a timely and useful fashion?
- lack of staff development on teaching and grading persuasive essays?

The variation in the potential causes of decreased student achievement highlight the importance of alignment.

The problem of curriculum design, therefore, must be integrated into the assessment, staff development, and management structures of a district if the district is to use curriculum as a tool for improving student achievement. All pieces of the definition of curriculum have to be in place for curriculum to affect student achievement. Ralph Tyler said it best:

> The primary educational function of organization is to relate the various learning experiences which together comprise the curriculum so as to produce the maximum cumulative effect in attaining the objectives of the school. The significant question to ask about any scheme of organization is: How adequately does it provide reinforcement of the several learning experiences so that they produce a maximum cumulative effect? (Tyler, 1977, p. 48)

We need to describe the powerful learning experiences (not just the goals) as part of a curriculum. Then the evaluation of those learning experiences provides the district with the opportunity to improve the alignment, the links between curriculum and assessment, so the structure can affect student achievement.

Does such a curriculum structure exist? Does it improve achievement? In the next section, I will describe how this curriculum definition structures a system of curriculum development, implementation, and refinement called the "Balanced Curriculum" and provide evidence that such a structure can dramatically affect student achievement because it systematically addresses alignment. Although the Balanced Curriculum is used as the model, I believe that any curriculum development system that incorporates all the major aspects of our definition and meets the ten criteria for a useful and usable curriculum (see Resource A) would theoretically produce similar results.

CRITERIA FOR A USEFUL AND USABLE CURRICULUM

In Resource A at the end of this book, I provide a rubric along with the following ten criteria for structuring a useful and usable curriculum:

1. Curriculum is useful and usable if it helps teachers use time to address content and pace instruction appropriately.

2. Curriculum is usable if the content is structured so that teachers know what is most important to teach and outlines how to teach the important content.

3. Curriculum is usable if teachers have the flexibility to use their own creativity when planning instruction.

4. Curriculum is useful if it focuses teacher instruction on the standards.

5. Curriculum is useful if it helps teachers balance their instruction so ideas aren't over- or underemphasized.

6. Curriculum is useful if it helps teachers and administrators know that students have performed at high levels on instruction aligned with standards and assessments.

7. Curriculum is useful and usable if the results of curriculum-embedded assessments can be compared with the results of state and standardized tests.

8. Curriculum is useful if it brings teachers together to collaborate on designing the curriculum and planning instruction.

9. Curriculum is useful if it has a structure for monitoring student and teacher completion of the curriculum.

10. Curriculum is usable if it is revised yearly to take into account the most recent performance on state or standardized tests (or both) and teachers' experience with the curriculum.

I would suggest that a district curriculum committee examine the five parts of the curriculum definition then commit the district's curriculum design to writing in a three- to five-page written document. The ten criteria can then be used to rate the district's curriculum design (using the rubrics in Resource A) to determine whether it will be powerful and efficient at producing improved student achievement, based on how it takes into account the alignment research. In the next chapter, I will model how to apply the ten criteria for structuring a useful and usable curriculum after showing how the Balanced Curriculum addresses alignment issues.

Addressing Alignment Through a Curriculum Design

The Balanced Curriculum Model

In the last chapter, we developed a definition of curriculum differing from the common definition and posed ten criteria for a useful and usable curriculum including attention to alignment. This chapter introduces the Balanced Curriculum model, one example of a curriculum design that brings the alignment pieces together in one system for curriculum development and implementation for school districts. The results from districts that wrote and implemented the Balanced Curriculum design show improved achievement in all cases where implementation was strong.

The Balanced Curriculum meets the definition of curriculum from the last chapter and fulfills the ten criteria for a useful and usable curriculum. The suggestions at the end of previous chapters can be combined into one curriculum system so that numerous strategies are not needed to ensure alignment. Because it is a curriculum system, the parts and pieces reinforce each other, thus ensuring alignment to the many facets of the alignment matrix.

Districts may have adopted many of these criteria in their curriculum design. If they are *not* getting significantly improved achievement, they may want to revisit their design to make sure all ten criteria are being met. The Balanced Curriculum is one model in which all of the ten criteria are met. All districts that have used the Balanced Curriculum design and ensured implementation have been rewarded with significantly improved achievement. Below are a few examples.

RESULTS FROM SCHOOL DISTRICTS USING CURRICULUM THAT MEETS THE TEN CRITERIA

Implementing the Balanced Curriculum approach can be the key to improved achievement. Data from the many schools and districts across the country that have used the Balanced Curriculum process to design their own curriculum shows that the process significantly improves achievement (Squires, 2005a, pp. 295–307). As Figure 9.1 demonstrates, school districts that both designed *and implemented* the curriculum saw their scores improve significantly (http://www.balancedcurriculum.com/results.htm).

Because the Balanced Curriculum operates from the Web with access determined by passwords, districts can save money through coordinated Web-based review and revision of their own curricula rather than via a paper-based process. Most districts can pay for the Web site access with the money they save in printing and publication costs.

In the last chapter we defined curriculum as a district's plan for guiding and aligning instruction. Student test performance improves because standards and standards-based assessment is ensured through staff development and district management of the curriculum. The findings suggest that districts can improve achievement by implementing a plan that:

1. structures curriculum to guide instruction (time, content, and process);

2. aligns curriculum content to standards and high-stakes tests;

3. assesses students on curriculum-based tasks and provides practice on high-stakes test formats;

4. ensures management of curriculum implementation, including staff development;

5. ensures management of data used to improve the curriculum.

These are the five major areas incorporated into the curriculum definition posed in Chapter 8.

(*Text continues on page 154*)

Figure 9.1 Results From Schools and Districts That Have Developed and Implemented the Balanced Curriculum

Place and Date	Subject	Grades	School Demographics	Results
Red Bank, NJ 1978–1992	R, LA, Math	K–8	800 approx. 60% Black 20% Hispanic 20% White 60% Free/Reduced lunch	Student averages at all grade levels went from below grade level to above grade level in R, LA, and Math over a period of seven years on a variety of standardized tests used by the district.
Richardson Elementary, Washington, DC 1993–1994	Reading	1–6	360 approx. 96% Black 100% Free/Reduced Lunch	Improvements pre implementation to post implementation. (Normal growth for a year's schooling is 1.0) Grade / Grade Equiv. Improvement 1–2 / .8 2–3 / 1.2 3–4 / –.6 4–5 / 1.2 5–6 / 1.1
Collection of New York City SURR Schools (schools under registration and review, i.e., declining scores for three years in a row) 1994 (Pre)–1997(Post)	Reading and Writing	K–6	1,000 (approx.) students per school Mostly high poverty, high minority schools	School/Grade — State Test % passing (Pre / Post) PS 191 Gr 3 Re 32.9 / 49.0 Gr 5 Wr 80.3 / 91.7 PS 165 Gr 3 Re 35.3 / 54.8 Gr 5 Wr 54.1 / 47.1 Gr 6 Re 74.5 / 66.7 PS 156 Gr 3 Re 26.9 / 72.2 Gr 5 Wr 47.1 / 77.6 PS 115 Gr 3 Re 68.0 / 75.6 Gr 5 Wr 94.8 / 90.3 PS 43 Gr 3 Re 48.8 / 54.7 Gr 5 Wr 75.6 / 90.0 Gr 6 Re 59.6 / 80.5 PS 15 Gr 3 Re 72.7 / 79.3 Gr 5 Wr 76.7 / 89.8 Gr 6 Re 79.4 / 79.0 PS 27 Gr 3 Re 34.9 / 57.4 Gr 5 Wr 89.6 / 78.9 Gr 6 Re 52.8 / 55.6 Yonkers Hostos/Micros Gr 3 Re 42 / 87 Gr 6 Re 36 / 62

(Continued)

Figure 9.1 (Continued)

Place and Date	Subject	Grades	School Demographics	Results
District 13 (Brooklyn, NY) 1997–2000	Reading	K–8	18 elementary 4 middle 1,000 students per school (Total 20,000 students) Mostly Black and poor	**Implementing Schools** Gained 7% more students scoring above grade level on city tests in Reading from previous year **Non-Implementing Schools** Lost 6% of students who scored above grade level on city tests in Reading from previous year
Newburgh, New York 1999–2002	Reading	K–8	6 elementary 2 middle Equal mix of White, Hispanic, and Black ES 350–800 MS 750–1,000	Fall to Spring Scores on District Standardized Test (expected growth = .6) LA (in Grade Equivalents) Gr. / Reading / LA 3 / 1.7 / 1.3 4 / 1.8 / 1.6 5 / 1.5 / 1.4 6 / 1.5 / 1.4 7 / .8 / .8 8 / .9 / .9
Passaic, NJ 2001–2003	Reading	K–8	8 elementary Mainly Hispanic and Black, primarily poor	Percent Proficient on Grade 4 State Test in Reading School / Pre / Post No. 1 / 67.6 / 84.8 No. 3 / 69.8 / 91.9 No. 5 / 43.9 / 64.1 No. 6 / 73.6 / 73.8 No. 9 / 64.9 / 73.5 No. 10 / NA / 57.1 No. 11 / 54.3 / 78.2 Learning Center / 94.1 / 95.0
Englewood Cliffs, NJ 2001–2004	Reading	K–8	1 elementary 1 middle 400 students in district upper middle class, large ESL population	**On State Test:** Level 1 = Below Proficient Level 2 = Proficient Level 3 = Above Proficient **Grade 8 State Test** Pre / Post 95% at Levels 1 & 2 / 71% at Levels 1 & 2 5% at Level 3 (highest) / 29% at Level 3 (highest) **Grade 4 State Test** Pre / Post 97% at Levels 1 & 2 / 20% at Levels 1 & 2 3% at Level 3 (highest) / 80% at Level 3 (highest)

Place and Date	Subject	Grades	School Demographics	Results
Hertford County, NC 2001–2004	Reading	K–8	Rural 70% Black 30% White	**State Test** Levels 3 & 4 (Proficient and Above) <div align="right">**% at Levels 3&4**</div> **Riverview Elementary** Grades 3 to Grade 4 improvement — +30.98% Grades 4 to Grade 5 improvement — +24.19% **Ahoskie Elementary** Grades 3 to Grade 4 improvement — −.71% Grades 4 to Grade 5 improvement — +24.13% **Hertford County Middle School** Grades 6 to Grade 7 improvement — +17.94% Grades 7 to Grade 8 improvement — +22.23%
Meriden Public Schools, CT 2005–2007 2006–2007 scores reported after first year of implementation	Math	K–5	8,900 total school population 8 elementary schools 15% Black 41% Hispanic 42% White 2% Other 56.5% Poverty (Only one school at one grade level declined; all other schools and grade levels increased)	**Results for 3–5 Math**

Results for 3–5 Math

District	Scores At or Above *Proficient* (3 or better on a 5 point scale)	Change
Gr 3 2006	54.8%	
Gr 4 2007	66%	
		11.2%
Gr 4 2006	60.4%	
Gr 5 2007	70.2%	
		9.8%

District	Scores At or Above *Goal* (4 or better on a 5 point scale)	Change
Gr 3 2006	26.2%	
Gr 4 2007	44.7%	
		18.5%
Gr 4 2006	40.3%	
Gr 5 2007	49.2%	
		8.9%

This chapter demonstrates how the Balanced Curriculum process uses the above curriculum components to meet the criteria for a useful and usable curriculum that improves achievement and includes attention to alignment issues. After I describe how the Balanced Curriculum works, I will explain how this curriculum structure affects student achievement and alignment. This chapter will end with a review of the ten criteria for a useful and usable curriculum.

The Balanced Curriculum is one model for development and implementation that uses the research about alignment to structure curriculum to improve student achievement on high-stakes tests. Many popular curriculum designs do not take the power of alignment into full consideration, including Wiggins and McTighe's *Understanding by Design* (2005), Erickson's Concept-Based Curriculum in *Stirring the Head, Heart, and Soul* (2001), Tomlinson's *Parallel Curriculum* (2002), Posner and Rudnitsky's *Course Design* (2006), and Jacobs' *Curriculum Mapping* (2004).

THE BALANCED CURRICULUM MODEL

Districts using the Balanced Curriculum Web site enter their curriculum information so that all teachers in the district have access to all the curriculum's components. The Balanced Curriculum has the following components:

- Courses
- Time-bound units
- Significant tasks (or assured activities)
- Alignment of significant tasks to standards and assessment
- Curriculum-embedded assessment aligned to state standards and assessment specifications
- A management system for tracking classes' progress
- A record of teachers' comments to guide staff development planning
- Yearly curriculum revision process

The following sections describe each component in detail.

Courses, Units, and Significant Tasks Guide Time, Content, and Process Dimensions of the Curriculum

The curriculum is written by the district's teacher-authors to guide instruction. Courses are divided into time-bound units so teachers know the pace of instruction. This ensures that everyone will complete the course's curriculum and students will not get left behind. Within the unit, significant tasks or assured activities, described by district teacher-authors in a paragraph, specify what district teachers should teach (an objective) and which instructional processes to use. The significant tasks take longer to complete than a daily lesson plan and generally encompass two days' to two weeks' worth of activities. The unit's significant tasks take approximately 60–70% of the unit's time. The other 30–40% is spent however the teacher decides to meet the class' needs, through remediation or enrichment or both. This allows teachers to retain the creative aspects of instruction.

Forty to sixty significant tasks usually make up a course. The significant tasks are the teacher's promise that most students will be ready for the following course or grade level. Figure 9.2 is a sample significant task for a high school English course.

Figure 9.2 Sample Significant Task for High School English

Students will set up an in-class debate to examine the controversial issues in *To Kill A Mockingbird*. They will have to take a stand on an issue and develop arguments to defend their positions. They will spend time examining the text and providing quotes as evidence to support their claims. They will be able to use their arguments in a structured debate format and setting. Students will give each other feedback on their debates using class generated rubrics.[1]

---

[1]Other examples of significant tasks can be found by going to www.balancedcurriculum.com using the User Name: SCSU Student, Password: 1234. There are over 200 courses there that have significant tasks developed for a vast variety of courses.

How Does the Curriculum Structure Affect Achievement and Alignment?

We know that students' prerequisite skills have a powerful effect on future learning (Bloom, 1976). If students enter a course with appropriate prerequisite skills, they are more likely to learn than if they lack the prerequisite skills. A district curriculum can ensure more students have those prerequisite skills by providing core or assured experiences (significant tasks) to which all students have equal access. Significant tasks also ensure that teachers are using a majority of their time teaching the most important content. This will not happen in a coordinated way without a curriculum (Walberg, 1988; Schmidt et al., 2001). Because the significant tasks are common across classrooms, when aligned to standards and assessments, they accurately reflect the "balance" of the curriculum.

Align to Standards and High-Stakes Assessment Specifications—Step 1

Alignment of curriculum to standards and high-stakes testing provides a powerful predictor of the curriculum's effect, as demonstrated by the many research studies cited in this book (e.g., Wishnick, 1989; Schmidt et al., 2001; Porter & Smithson, 2001). The curriculum authors align significant tasks to state standards and high-stakes assessment specifications. The vocabulary from the standards is explicitly incorporated into the significant tasks. Then the Web site generates a report showing the alignments for each significant task. Figure 9.3 illustrates how a significant task about a "Portfolio Project" is aligned to Connecticut's standards and state test blueprints. (The Web site contains all state and national standards, as well as local standards or a district's power standards for all enrollees.)

In Figure 9.3 the significant task is listed at the top. The first column lists the state standards and assessment specifications that the authors aligned to the significant task. For example, CAPT (Connecticut Academic Performance Test) Grade 10 Response to Literature is the state assessment specification for the part of the reading test for the state. The second column contains the state's code for this assessment specification. The third column lists what the state includes in that item. For example, in the area of CAPT 10—Editing and Revising, commas in a series, tone, misplaced modifiers, and proper notes are all aligned to the significant task. The curriculum authors debated among themselves and came to a consensus about the most important areas for alignment with the significant task.

How Does the Alignment Strategy Affect Achievement and Alignment?

Each significant task is taught by every teacher, using his or her unique style and teaching processes. Districts can be assured that standards aligned to the significant tasks are covered. The variability across teachers is decreased, while still allowing teachers to teach the significant task in ways that fit their style. This ensures alignment because the significant tasks cover the standards and the state test specifications.

Figure 9.3   Alignment of the Significant Task to the
Standards and the Assessment Specifications

Portfolio Project

Students will create a portfolio based on the reading of the book, *Speak*. As they read, they will respond to different issues in different types of writing assignments, while discussing in their journal how they handle new vocabulary words. They will have to write creative letters that will explain the thoughts of certain characters, essays that analyze theme, and summaries that explain major happenings in the book. Editing groups will work on commas in a series, fragments, misplaced modifiers, and proper nouns.

Standard	Code	Description
Bloom's Taxonomy	An	Analysis
	S	Synthesis
CAPT* Grade 10 – Response to Lit.	CAPT1.2	Does the student describe the thoughts, opinions, and/or questions that arise as he or she reads the story?
	CAPT2.1	Does the student use clues or evidence from the story to make inferences, draw conclusions, predict events, and infer motives and generalizations beyond the text?
	CAPT3.2	Does the student apply his or her understanding of people and life in general to make associations between the story and his or her view of the world?
	CAPT 4.4	Does the student examine the fit between the text of the story and his or her prior knowledge and life experience, and attempt to reconcile differences if appropriate?
CAPT Grade 10 – Editing and Revising	CAPT 1.1a	Commas in a series
	CAPT 1.5	Tone
	CAPT 2.1	Fragment
	CAPT 3.4	Misplaced Modifier
	CAPT 4.2	Proper Nouns
CT Language Arts Standards	912.01.02	Students will examine the fit between the text and prior knowledge by recording differences, extracting clues or evidence, making inferences, drawing conclusions, predicting events, inferring motives, and generalizing beyond the text.
	912.01.08	Students will apply their understanding of textual features of each genre to their interpretation of that genre.
	912.01.09	Students use word recognition strategies to perfect reading fluency in ever more sophisticated words.
	912.02.01	Students will select from the complete variety of text structures (essay, short story, poetry, academic essay, report, research paper, response to literature, documentary, etc.) the appropriate organizational pattern for addressing audience, purpose, and point of view.

*CAPT = Connecticut Academic Performance Test

Figure 9.4   Alignment of Connecticut Test Specifications to Significant Tasks

CAPT* Grade 10 – Response to Literature: Forming an Initial Understanding

CAPT 1.1 = Topic Sentence

Unit	Significant Task Title
Search for Self	Balanced Person
Survival	Physical/Mental Survival
Power	Power Structures
CAPT	CAPT Preparation

CAPT 1.2 = Supportive Detail

Unit	Significant Task Title
Search for Self	Records of Daily Life
Short Story	Unified Effect
Betrayal	Poster Project

CAPT 1.5 = Tone

Unit	Significant Task Title
Search for Self	Portfolio Project

*CAPT = Connecticut Academic Performance Test

Align to Standards and High-Stakes Assessment Specifications—Step 2: Balancing the Aligned Curriculum

Next, the alignments are summarized by course so the teacher-authors can determine if the balance among the standards is appropriate.

Figure 9.4 shows that for the CAPT (Connecticut Academic Performance Test), four significant tasks in four different units were aligned to the "Topic Sentence" content area on the state test. For "Supportive Detail" there were three significant tasks in three different units. For "Tone" there was one significant task in one unit aligned to this area of the test.

Teacher-authors may use Figure 9.4 to consider whether one significant task on tone (CAPT 1.5) provides sufficient emphasis for ninth-grade English, as only one significant task is aligned to the standard for tone. Curriculum teacher-authors use their professional judgments, as well as item analysis of district test scores, to support their decisions. For example, if students in the district didn't do well on the items testing tone on the state test, then the curriculum authors may want to add more significant tasks in other units which address tone. On the other hand, if the test results on tone were satisfactory, they may decide not to change it. This helps maintain teacher autonomy while ensuring standards are met.

Another report (see Figure 9.5) shows the number of significant tasks addressed by each standard and sub-standard. For example, look at the second standard listed in Figure 9.5 (K4.02.02). In the first column, the numeral *3* indicates that there are three significant tasks aligned to this standard. The standard is given in the third column.

Figure 9.5   Report of Number of Significant Tasks for the Course Aligned to Significant Tasks

Grade Two Number of Significant Tasks Aligned to Standards		2006–2007
Standard: CT Language Arts 2003 K–4		
Students will produce written, oral, and visual texts to express, develop, and substantiate ideas and experiences.		
	K4.02.01	Students will decide upon purpose, audience, and point of view, then select from a group of text types, such as narrative, nonfiction, and poetry, the most appropriate genre to convey their meaning.
3	K4.02.02	Students will speak, write, or draw in a variety of modes (narratives, "all-about" nonfiction pieces, poetry) to tell stories that their audience understands.
1	K4.02.03	Students will generate questions for gathering data from appropriate first-hand, visual, and print sources, and categorize the data to produce a product.
5	K4.02.04	Students will compose a piece of writing based on ideas generated through any of a variety of ways (writing, drawing, talking, webbing, listing, brainstorming) revise and proofread it, and present it to an audience.
	K4.02.05	Students will collect and examine, individually or with classmates, an array of their own stories and drawings, discuss the features they like, and say what they might do differently the next time.

The curriculum authors can use this report to ask questions about inadequate alignment and overemphasized alignment.

Inadequate Alignment

After reviewing Figure 9.5, the curriculum authors might ask, Why are there no significant tasks addressing the first standard and last standard in this section? Does the curriculum (via significant tasks) actually address these areas but they were not aligned because other alignments took priority? Was the alignment miscoded? Or did the curriculum (significant tasks) ignore these areas (usually inadvertently) and code others in its place? Do we as authors want to add or modify significant tasks so these areas can be addressed?

Overemphasized Alignment

The curriculum authors will need to decide whether standard K4.02.04, which is aligned to five significant tasks, is overemphasized given that two other standards (K4.02.01 and K4.02.05) have not been addressed at all. The curriculum authors will need to decide whether alignment to five significant tasks is too many. They may reason that because of the emphasis in the state test, coverage is necessary for the five significant tasks. Conversely, they could reason that such emphasis is inappropriate given the unaligned standards. Significant tasks may need to be rewritten for appropriate alignment. This ensures that all the significant tasks address the standards and assessment specifications in ways that the district's curriculum authors know is appropriate.

How Does the Alignment Strategy Affect Achievement and Alignment?

Students cannot learn what has not been taught (Schmidt et al., 2001). Aggregating alignment data by course ensures that the course design covers the standards and assessment specifications. The curriculum has power because the significant tasks, aligned to the standards and assessment specifications, are taught to all students. Therefore, students need access to instruction and time on topics required to meet the standards and achieve good test scores. Although all significant tasks are aligned individually, the power of alignment to improve achievement can only be determined through aggregating alignment information by course, not by individual tasks or lesson plans. The balance across the course is the most important indicator of improved achievement.

Assessing the Curriculum

Each significant task provides an opportunity for assessment. As the significant tasks are aligned to the standards, the assessment automatically covers similar territory. Teacher-authors construct a performance assessment for each significant task, so students have a standard way of demonstrating performance and teachers have a uniform way of grading the performance. The data from the assessments provide the district with comparable information about students' competence on the significant tasks and also indicates how well they performed on the aligned standards. The district can use assessment reports aggregated by school, task, or aligned standards. Such data can be used in recommending improvements to the curriculum.

Another type of assessment, the format assessment, provides all students with the once-per-unit opportunity to practice using a quiz that has the same format as the high-stakes state test. As the format assessments usually occur at the end of units, extensive test preparation is no longer necessary before the high-stakes test. Spaced practice is a better way to learn to take tests than intensive, often anxiety-provoking, practice right before the state assessment.

How Does Assessment Data Affect Achievement and Alignment?

The research suggests that students who have demonstrated competency on areas of the high-stakes test before taking the test are likely to do better than those who do not have the prerequisite skills. Likewise, students that understand the format of the test tend to do better than those who do not (Cohen, 1987).

The assessments help to determine whether students who do well on the significant tasks and format assessments will then do well on the high-stakes test. Since the district now has data, it can figure out whether this connection is strong or weak and modify the curriculum accordingly. Thus data drives the curriculum changes, built on the aligned assessments. For example, results of the content assessments, which test students' competence on particular standards, can be aligned with the district results from the state test provided that the state test reports this information so data can be compared. If the results on the content assessment are strong, but the results on the items from the state test are weak, then curriculum authors will need to decide if the significant task is strong enough.

Implementing the Curriculum

The district must plan strategies to ensure that the curriculum is actually implemented by the district's teachers and that teachers are actually teaching the significant tasks. This helps address teacher accountability. Because all teachers use the same significant tasks for a course, tracking a teacher's progress is a matter of determining if the significant tasks are taught. On the Balanced Curriculum Web site where the curriculum is located, teachers can log in to check off completion of a significant task and view their own completion record, but they cannot view other's completion records. Principals can check the progress of all teachers in their buildings. District staff can access completion information across district schools. This provides easily accessible information for managing student learning without micromanaging teachers' instruction.

How Does Implementation Affect Achievement and Alignment?

Ensuring that the units and significant tasks are taught guarantees all students access to content aligned to standards and high-stakes tests. It provides the next course's teacher with students whose prerequisite skills are similar. Principals now have a defined role in curriculum implementation: helping teacher groups implement the curriculum and monitoring progress to ensure that teachers complete the curriculum. They have data at their fingertips through access to up-to-the-minute reports from the Balanced Curriculum Web site to complete the job. Grade-level or course-level teams can also organize to assist each other with curriculum implementation discussions, thus fostering teamwork among the staff.

Modifying the Curriculum

The curriculum plan now generates data, so the curriculum can be modified based on the data. When modifying the curriculum, teachers and administrators need to ask questions about the data such as those shown in Figure 9.6.

Figure 9.6 Using Data Generated by Curriculum Implementation

Data Source	Questions Data Can Help to Answer
Alignment of Significant Task to Standards	Are all standard areas covered?
The Balance of the Curriculum	Does the existing balance of alignment with the standards promote increased achievement?
Significant Task Assessments	Do significant task assessments align with high-stakes assessments?
Format Assessments	Do format assessments align with high-stakes assessments?
Completion Information	Which significant tasks had low/high completion ratings? Did these correlate with test results?
High-Stakes/Standardized Test Results	For areas of low results, should the district increase emphasis on that area through more significant tasks and/or more time devoted to the aligned units/significant tasks?

How Does Modifying the Curriculum Affect Achievement and Alignment?

If the units and significant tasks are modified, then the alignments and assessments need to be modified also. Curriculum authors will need to determine whether the changes affect the balance and whether there now is an over- or underemphasis of particular standards in the curriculum.

Achievement can be positively affected if test results can be used to determine what curricular modifications to make. If main idea was an area in need of improvement, then more emphasis on that topic in the form of more time or more significant tasks needs to be employed. The sixty-percent time rule also needs to be taken into account so that the curriculum doesn't become stuffed with curriculum that takes too much time to accomplish. All these decisions rest on the judgment of the curriculum author team that is modifying the curriculum—a job for the best and the brightest minds in the district.

IS THE BALANCED CURRICULUM USEFUL AND USABLE?

In the last chapter I proposed ten criteria for a useful and usable curriculum, emphasizing alignment. Let's review that now to see how the Balanced Curriculum meets those ten criteria.

1. *Curriculum is useful and usable if it helps teachers use time to address content and pace instruction appropriately.*

   The units, with their unit introductions, provide an overview of the content contained in the unit and a specific time frame that indicates begin and end dates for pacing each unit. Teachers can record their completions of significant tasks on the Web site. School and district leaders can view reports that show how individual schools or the district as a whole is proceeding on implementing the curriculum. Important content is addressed through the significant tasks.

2. *Curriculum is usable if the content is structured so that teachers know what is most important to teach and outlines how to teach important content.*

   The significant tasks provide teachers with the content of what is important as well as a paragraph-length outline of an effective way to present the content developed by the curriculum authors from the district. The significant tasks use 60–70 % of the unit's time, allowing teachers time for remediation and enrichment depending on students' needs. Everyone presents the significant tasks, although individual interpretation is encouraged. Feedback from schools implementing the Balanced Curriculum suggests that new teachers appreciate the strong instructional models and processes incorporated into the significant tasks; it allows new teachers to learn powerful ways to teach the content sooner rather than discovering powerful and appropriate methods on their own. The significant tasks reduce teacher variation, because everyone teaches using these strong instructional models.

3. *Curriculum is usable if teachers have the flexibility to use their own creativity when planning instruction.*

   Although the significant tasks, or assured activities, are used by everyone, teachers can present the significant tasks in whatever order makes sense to them in each unit. They can also interpret the significant tasks in different ways to allow them to incorporate their own styles of teaching with the significant tasks. Finally, teachers can comment on the significant tasks and units so that their individual suggestions can be incorporated into the curriculum when it is revised.

4. *Curriculum is useful if it focuses teacher instruction on the standards.*

   Because the significant tasks are aligned to the standards, when the teachers teach the significant tasks, they are automatically helping students meet the standards. And because everyone teaches the significant tasks, administrators can be confident that all students will meet the standards. Because the significant tasks take up 60-70% of the curriculum's time, 60-70% of a teacher's instructional time is focused on the standards.

5. *Curriculum is useful if it helps teachers balance their instruction so ideas aren't over- or underemphasized.*

   The alignments are summarized by course for the district's curriculum authors. The curriculum authors determine what standards are over- or underemphasized and make appropriate adjustments. These judgments can be made on a yearly basis, taking into account the most recent state test scores, significant task completion data, and suggestions from the course teachers about improving the curriculum. The curriculum can be easily rebalanced using this data so that the emphasis is always up to date. For example, let's say a district was not performing well in the area of main idea. The curriculum authors rebalanced the curriculum by emphasizing main idea in an increased number of significant tasks to emphasize the concept throughout the curriculum. Their efforts paid off: scores on main idea improved. But scores still remained subpar on persuasive essays. The curriculum authors again rebalanced the curriculum by not putting quite as much emphasis on main idea and by replacing some significant tasks with more emphasis on persuasive essays. They received reports back from the Web site that the curriculum authors judged to be satisfactory in emphasizing persuasive essay while maintaining an emphasis on main idea.

6. *Curriculum is useful if it helps teachers and administrators know that students have performed at high levels on instruction aligned with standards and assessments.*

   As the significant tasks changed, so too did the content and format assessments. By collecting the results of the assessments aligned with main idea and persuasive essays, teachers and administrators were able to determine how well students were doing on those topics. Teachers also placed comments about whether they felt the significant tasks were strong enough.

7. *Curriculum is useful and usable if the results of curriculum-embedded assessments can be compared with the results of state and standardized tests.*

   When the new state assessment results are returned to the district, teachers, curriculum authors, and administrators can see if high scores on the content assessments predicted the results on the state assessments. If students scored well on the content assessments but did not do well on the state assessments, the curriculum authors could hypothesize. They might wonder whether the content assessments were too easy, or whether the content assessments were aligned to the assessment processes used by the state. Curriculum authors can examine the curriculum to see if enough significant tasks addressed the content of the state assessments. Curriculum authors can also determine if students had an adequate opportunity for review of the content. Although many factors affect the outcome of state tests, having a curriculum such as the Balanced Curriculum in place provides the data necessary to make an educated guess about how to address the problem.

8. *Curriculum is useful if it brings teachers together to collaborate on designing the curriculum and planning instruction.*

The Balanced Curriculum uses the best teachers in the district to construct and modify the curriculum. These teachers generally work in groups to design the curriculum, the units, and the significant tasks, and to assign the alignments and generate the assessments. Teamwork ensures that experienced teachers share their best knowledge of the craft with others throughout the district. Their knowledge of the craft is doubly powerful because it has been aligned with the standards and balanced to meet the needs of the district's students. The Balanced Curriculum encourages the institutionalization of knowledge of the craft by incorporating it into the district's significant tasks. Curriculum development is also staff development.

9. *Curriculum is useful if it has a structure for monitoring student and teacher completion of the curriculum.*

Teachers record the completion date for each significant task. Reports from the Web site can tell teacher leaders, principals, and central office staff (depending on their access level) how teachers are doing in completing the significant tasks in the curriculum. Principals and other administrators can become instructional leaders by helping to solve problems presented by teachers who fall behind or accelerate ahead of the begin and end dates of units. Grade-level or course-level meetings can then be exchanges of ideas about the best alternatives for teaching significant tasks or discussions of the implications of assessment results.

10. *Curriculum is usable if it is revised yearly to take into account the most recent performance on state or standardized tests (or both) and teachers' experience with the curriculum.*

Criteria six and seven demonstrate how state assessment results can be used to improve the curriculum. Curriculum authors examine the state test data for performance patterns. For areas of strong performance, curriculum authors consider whether the curriculum should de-emphasize these areas so that areas of need can use the time. For areas of weak performance, the curriculum can be re-aligned so that more emphasis is placed on these areas. Given that there may be many areas of weak performance, curriculum authors must decide which areas are most important to emphasize in the next year, taking into account what was emphasized in previous years. The Balanced Curriculum uses data from teacher comments, state tests, and results of content assessments to inform curriculum authors' judgments about changing the curriculum.

WHAT DISTRICTS CAN DO—A CONCLUSION

#9–1

Design, write, and implement a curriculum for the district that meets the ten criteria for a useful and usable curriculum.

This book demonstrates that alignment is important. Although there are many ways for districts to address alignment, the most powerful way is to design a curriculum structure that integrates alignment processes into curriculum development efforts. The results from the Balanced Curriculum suggest that district results on state and standardized assessments improve dramatically when alignment to state standards and assessments is a part of curriculum development and implementation (see Figure 9.1). When alignment's power is captured through curriculum development and implementation, student achievement improves.

How the Balanced Curriculum Meets This Book's Recommendations for Districts

SUMMARY OF RECOMMENDATIONS

This book contains thirty-one recommendations for districts to use to improve alignment. Those recommendations are summarized here along with an explanation of how they can be structured and addressed with curriculum design, using the Balanced Curriculum model specifically. The Balanced Curriculum model provides districts with a systematic framework for accomplishing most of these recommendations. Each recommendation is labeled with a chapter number first, then the number of the recommendation from that chapter.

#2–1

Use Porter's descriptors of instruction in math and science for high school to catalogue what instruction occurs. Align the descriptors with the state test specifications. Confirm that coverage of tested topics improves achievement.

The Balanced Curriculum uses the alignment of significant tasks to state standards and state assessments. Reports conducted by representative teachers are provided on the Balanced Curriculum Web site to confirm the alignment and balance. Because state standards and assessment specifications have already been loaded on the Web site, there is no need for generic descriptors of subject areas.

#2–2

Use the Survey of the Enacted Curriculum as a staff development process to compare instruction with standards and state assessments.

The significant tasks provide the same type of data as the Survey of the Enacted Curriculum, but they already are part of the curriculum development process instead of an addition. The Survey of the Enacted Curriculum could be used to augment the data from the Web site on teacher completion of the significant tasks. Data about completions could be triangulated with data from the Survey of the Enacted Curriculum and the results of state tests to determine areas where the curriculum needs to be refined.

#2–3

Rank test results by standards through released test items.

The alignment of significant tasks to assessment specifications provides a way to know where the curriculum needs to be improved based on the results of state testing. Because there is a curriculum with significant tasks that all teachers for a course agree to teach and assess, districts can be assured that the assessment specifications are covered in the curriculum. Where the results aren't adequate, the significant tasks (the curriculum) can be modified and strengthened.

#2–4

Provide teachers with opportunities to refine the scope and sequence of courses (especially for science lecture and lab activities), taking into account problematic areas of standards.

The units and the significant tasks define the scope and sequence of the courses. The significant tasks are aligned with the standards and assessment specifications. This means that once problematic areas are identified, they can be redesigned or refocused to take into account problematic areas of the standards and assessments.

#3–1

Coverage isn't enough—gather data on student practice opportunities in textbooks.

This recommendation is particularly important for a district that is textbook-driven, because the amount of practice provided for each concept is important for promoting good scores on the state test. The Balanced Curriculum is not driven by textbooks, rather by significant tasks aligned to standards and assessments, thereby ensuring that there will be enough practice opportunities for students related to the state's assessment.

#3–2

Conduct textbook alignment studies keyed to test results.

Again, the Balanced Curriculum is not textbook-driven but based on significant tasks. The significant tasks are aligned to the test specifications, making textbook analysis unnecessary. Textbooks can be referenced in the "Resources" section of the Balanced Curriculum Web site, so teachers know of the resources that can be used to complete the units and significant tasks. Textbook alignment studies can be completed to demonstrate that portions of the textbook will assist in the completion of significant tasks.

#3–3

Preview textbook purchases by analyzing practice opportunities for areas of weakness.

Textbooks are used as a resource rather than the actual curriculum; the significant tasks ensure adequate coverage. If the coverage is inadequate, as determined by test results or the alignment reports, the significant tasks can be modified, expanded, or eliminated. Textbook purchases need to be analyzed in terms of how they support the accomplishment of the district's significant tasks. (It may be that as districts add attachments to the Balanced Curriculum, the need for textbooks can be reduced, saving money that can then be spent on staff development to modify and improve the curriculum.)

#3–4

Survey teachers to determine the time spent on textbook topics before establishing district guidelines of time to be spent on topics.

The same activity can be part of the curriculum development process, as teams of district teachers establish the units and write the unit introductions. The curriculum development process provides a way to constructively use this data and compare it to the district's strengths and needs on state assessments.

#4–1

Lobby the state to provide adequate information on standards and alignment.

In order for results from statewide testing to be most useful, states need to report results to pupils, schools, and districts based on the major sections of the standards. States that do not provide this information are leaving pupils, schools, and districts without the data necessary to know where and how to improve their program. States reporting only one score on a test, thus saving money through shortchanging the test development process to include major sections of the standards, cheat pupils, schools, and districts of necessary data to use in improving their outcomes.

#4–2

Examine the alignment between the standards, the test specifications, and the reports generated by the test.

This activity is covered when teacher teams align their significant tasks to both the state standards and the state assessments, then use the results to balance the curriculum, ensuring appropriate emphasis given the test specifications and the standards in general.

#4–3

State professional organizations could replicate Webb's study using the WAT (Web Alignment Tool) and publish the results.

This recommendation would be helpful in the Balanced Curriculum process, but it is not part of the curriculum design. States should provide districts with this critical alignment information, especially as it is easily generated in a valid and reliable fashion.

#4–4

School districts should require schools to use state testing data to plan improvements.

The Balanced Curriculum is designed to be modified on a yearly basis using the district and school results of state testing, teacher comments on units and significant tasks from the Web site, and results from the assessments of the significant tasks.

#4–5

Set multiyear goals for district performance on state tests.

The curriculum itself provides a way to institutionalize a district's best in the units, significant tasks, alignments, and assessments. Through yearly goal setting, using feedback from teacher's comments, the district can reach a focused consensus on where improvements need to be made—the significant tasks, the curriculum-embedded assessments, or the balance in the alignment.

#4–6

Lobby the state to use Achieve's Ten Criteria for Essential Elements of a State's Longitudinal Data System.

Curriculum will be more effective if a state's test result information system is structured in a way that provides districts with necessary information (like results disaggregated by standards) so that districts can have in-depth knowledge of how students performed in sub-areas of the assessments. One individual score per tested area is not specific enough to assist in improving curriculum.

#4–7

Backload the curriculum: Align released test items with curriculum and textbooks.

The Balanced Curriculum aligns the significant tasks to state test specifications, thus eliminating the need to backload the curriculum.

#5–1

Implement a mastery learning model districtwide.

Implementing a mastery learning model requires a curriculum that specifies how time, content, and process will be integrated along with the needed assessments for the formative and summative unit assessments. It is possible to adapt the assessment specifications for a mastery learning model to the Balanced Curriculum design.

#5–2

Develop standard ways to periodically assess and reteach students.

The Balanced Curriculum includes assessments for each significant task and format (or end of unit) assessments that provide feedback to students and a data structure by which reteaching, part of the mastery learning model, can be provided.

#5–3

Provide feedback to students on a regular basis while providing itera-tive ways for students to demonstrate competence on learning tasks.

As stated above, the Balanced Curriculum does not explicitly include this, but could be easily modified so that there were two assessments for each significant task: one for assessing initial mastery after the first instruction, and a final mastery test for those students who did not pass the first mastery test. This would be given after other instruction was pro-vided by the teacher.

#6–1

Clarify benchmarks.

What the standards mean for instruction is clarified through the development of the significant task. The significant task details both the objective of instruction and the instructional process that the teacher-author teams determine is the strongest approach. The standards are clarified in the development and refinement of the significant tasks.

#6–2

Unburden the curriculum.

Rather than approach standards as yet another set of goals to accom-plish, standards could be approached as a systematic way to unburden the curriculum by identifying topics and concepts that are not mentioned in the standards but take time to accomplish in the curriculum. The align-ment and balancing of the Balanced Curriculum provide a way to unbur-den the curriculum during the curriculum development process.

#6–3

Cut major topics.

Time can be saved by following the recommendations for cutting top-ics in math and science as recommended by the American Association for the Advancement of Science (AAAS). Such recommendations can be addressed in the Balanced Curriculum development process where courses and units are designed. Such efforts will require additional staff develop-ment time, so curriculum authors understand the problem.

#6–4

Trim technical vocabulary.

The design of significant tasks can be a way to trim technical vocabulary, although not explicitly a part of the Balanced Curriculum design.

#6–5

Reduce wasteful repetition.

In the Balanced Curriculum development process, courses, units, and unit introductions are developed as a first step. Then curriculum authors, usually veteran teachers from the district, meet across courses to identify the gaps and repeated topics and concepts. Thus, reducing wasteful repetition is built into the curriculum development process.

#6–6

Learn to analyze curriculum materials.

Curriculum authors learn about developing units, significant tasks, and assessments as well as the alignment process. These employ all the skills needed to analyze curriculum materials. Curriculum authors match curriculum materials to the significant tasks.

#6–7

Align assessment to curriculum.

Many of these recommendations involve aligning assessment to curriculum. The Balanced Curriculum's structure, in which significant tasks are aligned to standards and assessments and the assessment of significant tasks is developed directly from the significant task description, ensures alignment of assessment and curriculum.

#6–8

Relate instructional units to strand maps.

One option for beginning curriculum development with the Balanced Curriculum in math and science is to use AAAS strand maps and circle the standards used in the units. Thus, adequate alignment has been addressed in developing the units even before the significant tasks have been developed.

#6–9

Create strand maps for other subject areas.
Strand maps can be created for other subject areas using existing state standards. This provides curriculum authors with a way to understand the standards before embarking on curriculum development. The strand maps can be used as described above for developing outlines of courses and units.

#7–1

Decide on fewer topics covered in more depth, particularly in math.
The design of significant tasks is one way that teachers can control the number of topics covered during a year. Significant tasks can be designed to build on one another, thus providing appropriate reinforcement and time to master important concepts.

#7–2

Develop districtwide tests, aligned to state assessments, to gain data on students' mastery of topics.
Districtwide assessment is already a part of the design of the Balanced Curriculum. Each significant task is assessed in such a way that results can be compared across classrooms. A format assessment, administered once per unit, is designed to provide students with practice with the format of the state's standardized assessment.

#7–3

Use test results to vary time and coverage of key topics.
You can determine whether to vary time and coverage of a topic only if there is a curriculum consensus on the content that is most important for students to cover and a plan (a curriculum) that spells out how much time is needed per topic. As part of the Balanced Curriculum development, curriculum author teams specify the units and their begin and end dates. After one year of curriculum implementation, results from state tests can be used to modify the amount of time spent on topics (part of balancing the curriculum).

#9–1

Design, write, and implement a curriculum for the district that meets the ten criteria for a useful and usable curriculum.

By now, you should be convinced that a curriculum that meets the above definition is the smartest way to combine many of these alignment strategies into a systematic approach specifying what students should know and be able to do so that teachers have the guidance to improve student achievement. There are other ways to structure a curriculum design. Let the dialogue begin.

Summary of Alignment Research and Recommendations

This chapter summarizes the book, presents all the research cited in the book on the alignment matrix, and presents two major conclusions based on the research.

SUMMARY OF THE BOOK

After an introductory chapter, the book examined the alignment side of curriculum alignment. The first four chapters reviewed the alignment research around three major areas: instruction, textbooks, and tests. These chapters emphasized the power of alignment of instruction, textbooks, and tests to other dimensions of schooling (written, taught, and tested curriculum) included in the alignment matrix. This established alignment as a powerful concept to be incorporated into a design for schooling.

In Part II, we extended our investigation into the curriculum part of curriculum alignment by examining curriculum systems such as mastery learning, Project 2061 for science and mathematics, and the research findings from a portion of the TIMSS and Schmidt et al. (2001). Together these curriculum systems demonstrate that the way curriculum is structured and organized has an effect on student performance.

Part III opened by investigating a definition of curriculum that includes alignment and posed ten criteria for a useful and usable curriculum that specifically incorporates aspects of alignment. After proposing the definition and criteria, we explored how the Balanced Curriculum (one way to structure curriculum while taking in many of alignment's aspects) meets the proposed definition of curriculum and meets the ten criteria for a useful and usable curriculum. This section demonstrated that appropriately structured curriculum is one way to capture alignment's power to improve student performance. The work of Schmidt et al. (2001) provided the research validation for this assertion. The improved test scores of district's that did a good job implementing the Balanced Curriculum demonstrate the power of an aligned curriculum to improve student performance on high-stakes tests.

SUMMARY OF THE BOOK'S CHAPTERS

What follows is a summary of each study and conclusions for each chapter (except Chapter 1 Introduction to Curriculum Alignment).

Chapter 2 Alignment and Instruction: Summary of Research

Porter et al. (1994) in the Reform Up Close study found that the content of instruction makes a difference in achievement.

Blank et al. (2001) found that alignment research is difficult to apply in urban settings because of central office indifference and teacher turnover. Where implementation was high, instruction was more closely aligned to state standards than in control schools. Implementation is a key variable in focusing the power of alignment.

McGehee and Griffith (2001) showed that improved achievement is a result of staff development on aligning instruction to state standards; however, implementation data was not part of the study.

DiBiase, Warren, and Wagner (2002) examined an effort to align chemistry lab instruction to lectures and national standards. Students were randomly assigned to groups taking the old course and students studying the new course. Student achievement improved for those taking the newly aligned course over the achievement of those taking the old course.

Chapter 2 Conclusions

Across the studies in this chapter, implementation and alignment of instruction and are two key variables that affect results. Time spent on content is a predictor of student achievement.

Chapter 3 Alignment and Textbooks: Summary of Research

Freeman et al. (1983) demonstrated that textbooks are inadequately aligned to standardized tests by showing that one-half to two-thirds of the topics covered by the standardized tests don't have twenty practice problems in the textbooks.

Howson (1995) concluded that U.S. textbooks cover over three hundred topics, too many to provide students with enough practice to understand the concepts, and little guidance for teachers as to which concepts should be emphasized the most.

Schmidt et al. (2001) showed that teachers use textbooks as one clue to determine what to emphasize. If the textbook covers a topic in depth, then teachers' will gear their instruction on that topic to be in depth.

Studies of textbooks conducted by the American Association for the Advancement of Science (AAAS) showed the alignment between quality instruction and the guidance provided by the textbooks to be of generally poor quality in math and science textbooks for middle and high school.

Goodman et al (1987) found misalignment between the content of reading textbooks for elementary school and good instruction, tests and the textbooks, and a lack of comprehension instruction.

Moss-Mitchell (1998) studied one large school district where the district had analyzed the textbook and provided instructional material for teachers on topics not covered by the textbook but presented in the state test. Student achievement improved as a result.

Price-Baugh's study (1997) showed that the number of practice items correlated to student scores on a state assessment.

Chapter 3 Conclusions

Textbooks aren't perfect: they may not be well aligned to standards and state or standardized assessments and may not have appropriate directions for teachers who want to deliver high-quality instruction. Yet textbooks are used by teachers to help determine what topics to emphasize. Two studies indicated that when a district can determine what textbooks emphasize and align this to the state assessment, while providing extra material for content not covered, student achievement can improve.

Chapter 4 Alignment of Standards and Standardized Tests: Summary of Research

Webb (1997) demonstrated a way to validly and reliably align state tests to state standards. Based on his analysis of four unnamed states, alignment ranged from acceptable to unacceptable. Webb's work set the standard for reliably and validly judging alignment between standards and tests.

Browder et al. (2004) showed another way to determine alignment of standards to assessments and demonstrated that special education tests were at times aligned to state standards.

Wise et al. (2006) and Wise and Alt (2006) used standards from Delaware to show how to ensure vertical alignment of standards between grade levels. Results indicated where the vertical alignment of standards in Delaware could be improved.

Quellmalz et al. (2006) used an alignment process to refine the meaning of a standard on science inquiry and showed how an expanded definition of science inquiry aligned with the items of three large-scale assessments, pointing out how the assessments could be structured to better assess science inquiry.

Bowe and Kingsbury (2007) and the National Center for Educational Statistics Study (2007) demonstrated that state tests are not equivalent, making the requirement of No Child Left Behind for 100% of the state's students to pass state tests by 2014 problematic.

English and Steffy (2001) suggest backloading the curriculum to include assessment items and instruction on those items that are aligned to the state test. No research validation was provided.

Next a model was proposed that showed what information a state should provide districts so that districts can align their curriculum to the state standards and assessments.

Chapter 4 Conclusions

The alignment between state assessments and state standards is problematic, because the standards cover all the important concepts students should know and be able to do, while state tests are constrained by testing time and can test only a limited number of concepts. There are now valid and reliable methods for determining the alignment between state assessments and state standards that can be used to improve this problematic condition. States should provide districts with data so that they are able to improve their instruction based on test data.

Chapter 5 Alignment, Reteaching, and Mastery Learning: Summary of Research

What the Bloom model showed us is that when curriculum, instruction, and lesson planning are aligned with curriculum-embedded tests (and there is a teach, test, reteach, test instructional model in place), student results can improve dramatically in the laboratory and in schools and districts that implement the model well.

Cohen's (1987) research demonstrated that when curriculum-embedded tests are aligned to instruction, student performance improves.

Wishnick (1989) showed that when curriculum-embedded tests are aligned with standardized tests, results improve and socioeconomic status, gender, and teacher are not important in predicting results.

Chapter 5 Conclusions

Mastery learning is a theory that has proven itself in lab settings and the real world of school districts. For mastery learning to be implemented, there needs to be alignment between instruction and assessment and a teach, test, reteach, test instructional model. Well implemented models of mastery learning contain many alignment components.

Chapter 6 Project 2061 of the American Association for the Advancement of Science (AAAS): Summary of Research and Conclusions

Based on AAAS's analysis, which relied on logical criteria rather than research studies, the following strategies can be used by districts:

- Clarify benchmarks.
- Unburden the curriculum.
- Cut major topics.
- Trim technical vocabulary.
- Reduce wasteful repetition.
- Learn to analyze curriculum materials.
- Align assessment to curriculum.
- Relate instructional units to strand maps.
- Create strand maps for other subject areas.

Chapter 7 Alignment and the TIMSS Analysis: Summary of Research and Conclusions

Schmidt et al. (2001) showed that the content of a country's curriculum affects student achievement in that country. This research validates curriculum as a crucial instrument in improving student achievement, as a school district has ultimate control over what students are taught and learn. If the curriculum is aligned with the assessment, results improve.

Chapter 8 Criteria for a Useful and Usable Curriculum: A Summary

Chapter 8 focused on criteria for curriculum design that encompasses many alignment concepts discussed in previous chapters. A definition of curriculum was proposed: *Curriculum is the district's written plan incorporating aspects of time use, content, and process aligned to standards and assessments that establishes a focus for instruction, assessment, staff development and management so student achievement improves.* This definition meets the ten criteria for a useful and usable curriculum.

Chapter 9 The Balanced Curriculum Model: A Summary

The Balanced Curriculum was presented as one model that meets the definition of curriculum proposed in Chapter 8 and that incorporates the many aspects of alignment explained in this book. Results from ten years of implementing the Balanced Curriculum in districts throughout the country indicate that student achievement will improve when the curriculum is developed using the Balanced Curriculum model and there are data suggesting high levels of implementation.

Chapter 10 How the Balanced Curriculum Meets This Book's Recommendations

The recommendations for improving alignment made throughout this book are gathered in Chapter 10 alongside an explanation of how the Balanced Curriculum Model addresses each recommendation.

Chapter 11 Summary of Alignment Research and Recommendations

After this summary of chapters, the book will conclude by placing all the research presented in the book on the alignment matrix.

THE RESEARCH POSTED ON THE ALIGNMENT MATRIX

All of the research cited in this book is placed on the alignment matrix in Figure 11.1, using the author codes below. Author codes are assigned by chapter, covering the major authors mentioned.

Figure 11.1 The Complete Alignment Matrix

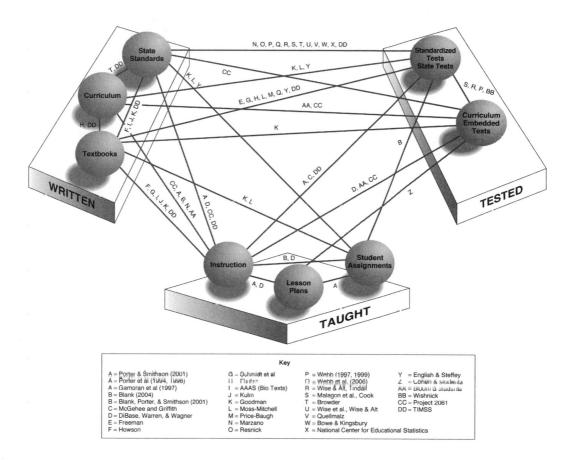

The research placed on the alignment matrix shows that:

- Most of the possible alignment areas have been studied. Lesson plans and student assignments are the least studied areas.
- Alignment between state standards and standardized or state tests is the most studied relationship, as findings in this area will have the most effect.

- As researchers have used many different definitions of curriculum focused around textbooks, standards, and instruction, there is a lack of research on how specific curriculum design or structure affects alignment and achievement, although the Balanced Curriculum model takes into account many of the dimensions of alignment and has demonstrated improved student achievement.
- More research is needed that is similar to DiBiase, Warren, and Wagner (2002) which was an excellent case study with random assignment of students which tested out two models (one aligned and one unaligned) for a chemistry course.

MAJOR FINDINGS FROM THE ALIGNMENT RESEARCH

There are two major findings from the alignment research reported in this book; commentary on each finding follows.

Findings

1. Alignment improves outcomes.

2. Alignment is a powerful research-based tool to incorporate into the design of the written, taught, and tested curriculum that guides instruction, assessment, and staff development.

Discussion

1. Alignment improves outcomes.

   Most of the areas on the alignment matrix, when aligned to other areas, have been associated with improved results. This demonstrates that alignment is a powerful tool for improving student achievement and leveling the playing field by reducing the power of socioeconomic status, race, gender, teacher assignment, and school size as predictors of student achievement. Well-designed instruction in which there is alignment among the written, taught, and tested curriculum can overcome traditional predictors of student achievement. Good instructional design can overcome students' backgrounds.

   This book argues that districts are the vehicle to carry this change by deciding what needs to be taught and aligning the taught, tested, and written curriculum to the states' standards and assessments. The Balanced Curriculum is proof that paying attention to alignment in curriculum structure, design, and implementation results in dramatic increases in test scores over a short period of time. This leads to the second conclusion.

2. Alignment is a powerful tool to incorporate into the design of the written, taught, and tested curriculum that guides instruction, assessment, and staff development.

Without alignment, the district's curriculum will not be coordinated with state standards and assessments, leading to random and uncoordinated efforts at improving student achievement. Some studies show how the written curriculum from a district can be structured to improve student achievement, such as the Balanced Curriculum process (Squires, 2005a) and the work of Schmidt et al. (2001), which demonstrates that when national curriculums are compared, results vary with the alignment among standards, the TIMSS assessment, teacher use of time, and textbook content.

In part, this is because district curriculums are so variable that there is little curriculum infrastructure that allows for comparison across districts. Because many districts don't realize that curriculum can be one way to systematize improvement of student achievement, districts typically adopt a potpourri of different programs and approaches, which may not fit together from a student's or teacher's perspective. Then "initiative fatigue" sets in as programs are adopted before previous adoptions can be fully implemented.

Districts can control their own destiny only if they have a way to plan and deliver what students should know and be able to do—the district curriculum. Districts realize that curriculum work can determine whether the parts and pieces of past program adoptions fit together into a coherent whole. The district curriculum provides a way to manage our expectations and resist the latest and greatest program if it does not fit within the existing structure.

What does a successful written district curriculum look like, one that is powerful enough to improve student achievement? What are its components? Why does it work? How can we make sure it is well implemented? We need to examine curriculum models, such as the Balanced Curriculum and others, that meet the criteria for a useful and usable curriculum so that we can understand how those models work. Some models will be more powerful than others.

The research cited in this book makes a case for alignment being an important aspect of curriculum design and poses many different ways that districts can tap some of alignment's power. Many curriculum designs make limited use of alignment (see for example Erickson [2001], Jacobs, [2004], and Wiggins & McTighe [2005]), yet they are very popular. Could these designs be even more powerful if they included aligning curriculum with standards and assessments?

The Balanced Curriculum, on the other hand, explicitly uses the power of alignment and has gotten dramatic results in districts that have designed and implemented the curriculum using the Balanced Curriculum design. I am not arguing one design's superiority over others, rather, that there needs to be a dialogue about design and the components of various curriculum systems. What allows them to work to produce improved achievement? Does this improvement have anything to do with other factors, such a district type (i.e., urban, suburban, or rural)? There must be design principles to follow toward creating a validated curriculum system that works in many districts. Districts are desperately looking for such a curriculum structure to deal with improvement pressures from No Child Left Behind. The definition of curriculum put forward in this book is an attempt to get the dialogue started.

Resource

Ten Criteria for Structuring a Useful and Usable Curriculum

1. Curriculum is useful and usable if it helps teachers use time to address content and pace instruction appropriately.

2. Curriculum is usable if the content is structured so that teachers know what is most important to teach and outlines how to teach important content.

3. Curriculum is usable if teachers have the flexibility to use their own creativity when planning instruction.

4. Curriculum is useful if it focuses teacher instruction on the standards.

5. Curriculum is useful if it helps teachers balance their instruction so ideas aren't over- or underemphasized.

6. Curriculum is useful if it helps teachers and administrators know that students have performed at high levels on instruction aligned with standards and assessments.

7. Curriculum is useful and usable if the results of curriculum-embedded assessments can be compared with results of state and standardized tests.

8. Curriculum is useful if it brings teachers together to collaborate on designing the curriculum and planning instruction.

9. Curriculum is useful if it has a structure for monitoring student and teacher completion of the curriculum.

10. Curriculum is usable if it is revised yearly to take into account the most recent performance on state or standardized tests (or both) and teachers' experience with the curriculum.

The rubric should help you to make systematic and thoughtful decisions about the structure of the curriculum for your district. I recommend tackling this task with a districtwide planning or steering committee prior to writing the curriculum. Coming to a consensus on the most appropriate design will build your capacity to implement the curriculum. After describing your curriculum, rate your design using the ten criteria for structuring a useful and usable curriculum along with the accompanying rubrics. You can download this work sheet and the criteria from the Balanced Curriculum Web site (www.balancedcurriculum.com).

RATE YOUR DESIGN

Directions: Now that you have put your design together, rate the design for usefulness and usability employing the following rubrics.

Ten Criteria for Structuring a Useful and Usable Curriculum

- Curriculum is useful and usable if it helps teachers use time to address content and pace instruction appropriately.

Needs Improvement	Emerging	Strong
The curriculum does not provide useful guidance about how much time to spend on curricular content.	The curriculum provides some guidance in planning time use during the school year.	The curriculum provides useful and specific guidance in planning time use during the school year.
Teachers would not know from the curriculum if they are spending too much or too little time on a topic.	Some general guidance is provided for how much time to spend on a topic.	The curriculum can help teachers determine if they are spending too much or too little time on a topic.

- Curriculum is usable if the content is structured so that teachers know what is most important to teach and outlines how to teach important content.

Needs Improvement	Emerging	Strong
Neither what to teach nor how to teach it is specified in the curriculum.	What to teach is specified but how to teach it is not.	Indications of what to teach and how to teach it are included in the curriculum.

- Curriculum is usable if teachers have the flexibility to use their own creativity when planning instruction.

Needs Improvement	Emerging	Strong
Teachers have complete flexibility because neither the curriculum content or instructional processes are provided in the curriculum.	While the curriculum specifies content, teachers have complete flexibility in determining how the content will be taught.	The curriculum specifies both content and process but at a general level so that teachers have flexibility in planning.

- Curriculum is useful if it focuses teacher instruction on the standards.

Needs Improvement	Emerging	Strong
The curriculum is aligned with neither standards nor assessments.	The curriculum is aligned with either standards or assessments, but not both.	The curriculum is aligned to both standards and assessments.
The alignment process is not specified or shown in the curriculum document.	The alignment process is specified in the curriculum document so readers know how the alignment process took place.	The alignment process is both specified and shown in the curriculum document. "Shown" means it is possible to make judgments about the alignment based on what is presented in the curriculum.

- Curriculum is useful if it helps teachers balance their instruction so ideas aren't over- or underemphasized.

Needs Improvement	Emerging	Strong
The curriculum gives no indication that appropriate weight was given to the standards and external assessments.	The curriculum asserts that there is an appropriate balance, but how that balance was achieved is not specified.	After alignment, the curriculum was balanced to provide appropriate coverage aligned to standards and external assessments.

- Curriculum is useful if it helps teachers and administrators know that students have performed at high levels on instruction aligned with standards and assessments.

Needs Improvement	Emerging	Strong
Curriculum-embedded assessments are not part of the curriculum.	There is a plan to make curriculum-embedded assessments part of the curriculum, such as common quarterly assessments.	Curriculum-embedded assessments are part of the curriculum. They specify what is assessed in each unit.
Curriculum-embedded assessments are not part of the curriculum.	Teachers have access to student performance data on curriculum-embedded assessments.	Both teachers and administrators have access to student performance data on curriculum-embedded assessments.

- Curriculum is useful and usable if the results of curriculum-embedded assessments can be compared with results of state and standardized tests.

Needs Improvement	Emerging	Strong
State scores do not give information for each standard or objective tested.	State scores do not give information for each standard or objective tested on the test. However, the district correlates scores on curriculum-embedded assessments with the scores on the tests.	The district has a way to prove that if students score high on the curriculum-embedded assessment, they will also score well on the state or standardized assessment.

- Curriculum is useful if it brings teachers together to collaborate on designing the curriculum and planning instruction.

Needs Improvement	Emerging	Strong
Only a few teachers were chosen because they were available at the time curriculum development occurred.	Curriculum development was done by a group of teachers that is not necessarily representative of all the schools in the district.	Curriculum development was done by a representative group of teachers with membership from each school in the district.
Teachers have no common planning period, so they get together infrequently to translate significant tasks into lesson plans.	Teachers have a common planning period but do not get together on grade- or course-level teams. Planning is done individually.	Teachers have common planning periods that they use to translate the significant tasks into lesson plans.

- Curriculum is useful if it has a structure for monitoring student and teacher completion of the curriculum.

Needs Improvement	Emerging	Strong
Teachers do not report their completion of the curriculum to anyone.	Teachers report their completion of the curriculum to the principal.	Teachers report their completion of the curriculum to the principal, who in turn reports it to the central office.
Student results from curriculum-embedded tests are not gathered.	The principal gathers student results from curriculum-embedded tests on a regular basis. The results aren't used to make changes in the curriculum.	The principal gathers student results from curriculum-embedded tests on a regular basis. The results are used to provide input to curriculum authors, who update the curriculum on a yearly basis.

- Curriculum is usable if it is revised yearly to take into account the most recent performance on state or standardized tests (or both) and teachers' experience with the curriculum.

Needs Improvement	Emerging	Strong
No data from testing information is used to update the curriculum. The curriculum, once written, is not updated regularly.	Data, such as item analysis from state and standardized tests, are used to update the curriculum at least every other year.	Data, such as item analysis from state and standardized tests, are used to update the curriculum on a yearly basis.
Teachers' experience with and recommendations for the curriculum are not recorded.	Teachers' experience with and recommendations for the curriculum are recorded, but the information is not used to update the curriculum.	Teachers' experience with and recommendations for the curriculum are recorded, and the information is used to update the curriculum on a yearly basis.

References

Achieve, Inc. (2001) *Creating a longitudinal data system: Using data to improve student achievement.* Retrieved March 3, 2006 from http://www.achieve.org/dstore.nsf/Lookup/DQC_paper/$file/DQC_paper.pdf

Ainsworth, L., & Viegut, D. (2006). *Common formative assessments: How to connect standards-based instruction and assessment.* Thousand Oaks, CA: Corwin Press.

Alexson, R., & Kemnitz, C. (2003). *Curriculum articulation and transitioning student success: Where are we going wrong and what lessons have we learned?* Paper presented at the Annual Meeting of the Association of American Geographers, New Orleans, LA.

American Association for the Advancement of Science. (1989). *Science for all Americans.* New York: Oxford University Press.

American Association for the Advancement of Science. (1993). *Benchmarks for science literacy.* New York: Oxford University Press.

American Association for the Advancement of Science. (2001). *Atlas for science literacy Volume 1.* New York.

American Association for the Advancement of Science. (2007). *Atlas for science literacy Volume 2.* New York.

American Association for the Advancement of Science. (2001). *Designs for science literacy.* New York: Oxford University Press.

Ananda, S. (2003). Achieving Alignment. *Leadership 33*(1), 18–21.

Anderson, L. W. (1973). *Time and School Learning.* Unpublished doctoral dissertation. University of Chicago, IL.

Anderson, L. W. (2002). Curricular alignment: A re-examination. *Theory into Practice, 41*(4), 255–260.

Anderson, L. (2005). Objectives, evaluation, and the improvement of education. *Studies in Educational Evaluation, 31*(2–3), 102.

Arlin, M. N. (1973) *Learning rate and learning rate variance under mastery learning conditions.* Unpublished doctoral dissertation. University of Chicago, IL.

Billig, S. H., Jaime, I. I., & Abrams, A. (2005). Closing the achievement gap: Lessons from successful schools. Washington, DC: U. S. Department of Education.

Binor, S. (1974). *The relative effectiveness of mastery learning strategies in second language acquisition.* Unpublished doctoral dissertation. University of Chicago, IL.

Blank, R. K., Porter, A., & Smithson, J. (2001). *New tools for analyzing teaching, curriculum and standards in mathematics & science: Results from survey of Enacted Curriculum Project.* Washington, DC: Council of Chief State School Officers.

Blank, R. K. (2002). Using surveys of enacted curriculum to advance evaluation of instruction in relation to standards. *Peabody Journal of Education, 77*(4), 86–120.

Blank, R. K. (2004). *Data on enacted curriculum study: Summary of findings.* Washington, DC: Council of Chief State School Officers.

Block, J. H. (1970). *The effects of various levels of performance on selected cognitive, affective and time variables.* Unpublished doctoral dissertation. University of Chicago.

Block, J. H. (Ed.). (1971). *Mastery Learning.* New York: Holt, Rinehart and Winston.

Block, J. H. (1974). Mastery learning in the classroom: An overview of recent research. In J. H. Block (Ed.), *School, society, and mastery learning* (pp. 28–69). New York: Holt, Rinehart and Winston.

Block, J. H., & Burns, R. B. (1976). Mastery learning. In L. S. Shulman (Ed.), *Review of research in education.* Itasca, IL: Peacock.

Block, J. H., Efthim, H. E., & Burns, R. B. (1989). *Building effective mastery learning schools.* New York: Longman.

Bloom, B. S. (1976). *Human characteristics and school learning.* New York: McGraw-Hill.

Bowe, B. P., & Kingsbury, G. G. (2007, April). *Comparison of four state performance standard alignment methods.* Paper presented at the American Educational Research Association, Chicago, IL.

Browder, D., Flowers, C., Ahigrim-Deizell, L., Karvonen, M., Spooner, F., & Algozzine, R. (2004). The alignment of alternate assessment content with academic and functional curricula. *Journal of Special Education, 30*(4), 211–223.

Carroll, J. B. (1963). A model of school learning. *Teacher's College Record, 64,* 723–733.

Clarke, N., Stow, S., Ruebling, C., & Kayona, F. (2006). Developing standards-based curricula and assessments: Lessons from the field. *Clearing House: A Journal of Educational Strategies, Issues and Ideas, 79*(6), 258.

Cohen, S. A., & Stover, G. (1981). Effects of teaching sixth grade students to modify the variables in math word problems. *Reading Research Quarterly, 16,* 175–200.

Cohen, S. A. (1987). Instructional alignment: Searching for a magic bullet. *Educational Researcher, 16,* 16–19.

Cook, G. H. (2006). Aligning English language proficiency tests to English language learning standards. In *Aligning assessment to guide the learning of all students. State collaborative on assessment and student standards.* Washington, DC: Council of Chief State School Officers.

Connecticut State Department of Education. (1999). Mathematics Connecticut Mastery Test Third Generation Mathematics Handbook, Part 1. Retrieved Feb. 1, 2008, from http://www.sde.ct.gov/sde/cwp/view.asp?a=2618&q=320878.

Council of Chief State School Officers, (May, 2000). *Using data on enacted curriculum in mathematics and science: Sample results from a study of classroom practices and subject content.* Washington, DC: Council of Chief State School Officers.

Council of Chief State School Officers. (2002). *Using data on enacted curriculum—A guide for professional development.* Washington, DC: Rolf K. Blank.

Council of Chief State School Officers. (2003). Using data on enacted curriculum: A professional development and technical assistance model for using the Survey of Enacted Curriculum. Retrieved August 21, 2005, from http://www.ccsso.org/content/pdfs/DECpdoverviewYR3Reprt.ppt#54

Council of Chief State School Officers. (2005). Surveys of enacted curriculum. Washington, DC: Council of Chief State School Officers. Retrieved August 21, 2005 from http://www.ccsso.org/projects/Alignment_Analysis.

Crocker, L., & Algina, J. (1986). *Introduction to classical and modern test theory.* New York: Harcourt Brace & Jovanovich.

Cronin, J. (2004). *Aligning the NWEA RIT scale with the California Standards Test (CST).* Lake Oswego: Northwest Evaluation Association.

DiBiase, W. J., Warren, J., & Wagner, E. P. (2002). Aligning general chemistry laboratory with a lecture at a large university. *School Science and Mathematics, 102,* 158–171.

Elia, J. S. I. (1986). *An alignment experiment in vocabulary instruction: Varying instructional practice and test item formats to measure transfer with low SES fourth graders.* Unpublished doctoral dissertation. University of San Francisco, CA.

English, F. W. (1992). Deciding what to teach and test: Developing, aligning, and auditing the curriculum. In F. W. English (Ed.). *Successful schools: Guidebooks to effective educational leadership: Vol. 4.* Newbury Park, CA: Corwin Press.

English, F. W., & Steffy, B. E. (2001). *Deep curriculum alignment: Creating a level playing field for all children on high-stakes tests of educational accountability.* Lanaham, MD: Scarecrow Press.

Erickson, H. L. (2001). *Stirring the head, heart, and soul: Redefining curriculum and instruction* (2nd ed.). Thousand Oaks, CA: Corwin Press.

Evans, S. M. (2002). Aligning to state standards. *Science Teacher 69*(3), 54–57.

Ewing, T. (2003). Aligning instruction to standards: A local approach. *Leadership, 32*(3), 30–31.

Fahey, P. A. (1986). *Learning transfer in main ideas instruction: Effects of instructional alignment on main idea test scores.* Unpublished doctoral dissertation. University of San Francisco, CA.

Floden, R. E., Porter, A. C., Schmidt, W.H., Freeman, D. J., & Schwille, J. R. (1980). Responses to curriculum pressures: A policy-capturing study of teacher decisions about content. *Journal of Educational Psychology, 73(2),* 129–141.

Freeman, D., Kuhs, T., Porter, A., Floden, R., Schmidt, W., & Schwille, J. (1983). Do textbooks and tests define a national curriculum in elementary school mathematics? *Elementary School Journal, 83,* 501–513.

Gentile, J. R., & Lalley, J. P. (2003). *Standards and mastery learning.* Thousand Oaks, CA: Corwin Press.

Gamoran, A., Porter, A. C., Smithson, J., White, P. A. (1997, Winter). Upgrading high school mathematics instruction: Improving learning opportunities for low-achieving, low income youth. *Education Evaluation and Policy Analysis, 19,* 325–338.

Goodman, K. S., Shannon, P., Freeman, Y. S., & Murphy, S. (1987). *Report card on basal readers.* Katonah, NY: Richard C. Owen.

Groves, F. H. (1995). Science vocabulary load of selected secondary science textbooks. *School Science and Mathematics, 95*(5), 231–235.

Guskey, T. R., & Pigott, T. D. (1988). Research on group-based mastery learning programs: A meta-analysis. *Journal of Educational Research, 81,* 197–216.

Hall, R., (2002). Aligning learning, teaching and assessment using the web: An evaluation of pedagogical approaches. *British Journal of Educational Technology, 33*(2), 149–158.

Howson, G. (1995). *Mathematics textbooks: A comparative study of grade 8 texts.* Vancouver, Canada: Pacific Education Press.

Jacobs, H. H. (1997). *Mapping the big picture; Integrating Curriculum & Assessment K–12.* Alexandria, VA: Association for Supervision and Curriculum Development.

Jacobs, H. H. (Ed.). (2004). *Getting results with curriculum mapping.* Alexandria, VA: Association of Supervision and Curriculum Development.

Kendall, J. S., & Marzano, R. J. (1997a). *A comprehensive guide to designing standards-based districts, schools and classrooms.* Alexandria, VA: Association for Supervision and Curriculum Development.

Kendall, J. S., & Marzano, R. J. (1997b). *Content knowledge: A compendium of standards and benchmarks for K–12 education.* Denver, CO: MCREL Lab.

Kozar, M. L. (1984). *Effects of varying degrees of instructional alignment in post-treatment tests on mastery learning tasks of fourth grade children.* Unpublished doctoral dissertation. University of San Francisco, CA.

Kulik, C. C., Kulik, J. A., & Bangert-Drowns, R. L. (1990). Effectiveness of mastery learning programs: A meta-analysis. *Review of Educational Research, 60*(2), 265–269.

Kulm, G., Roseman, J., & Treistman, M. (1999). A benchmarks-based approach to textbook evaluation. *Science Books & Films, 3,5,*147–153.

La Marca, P. M. (2001). Alignment of standards and assessments as an accountability criterion. *Practical Assessment, Research & Evaluation, 7*(21).

Levin, T. (1975). *The effect of content prerequisite and process-oriented experiences on application ability in the learning of probability.* Unpublished doctoral dissertation. University of Chicago, IL.

Levine, D. U. and associates. (1985). *Improving student achievement through mastery learning programs.* San Francisco: Jossey-Bass.

Lawson, A., Bordingnon, C., & Nagy, P. (2002). Matching the Grade 8 TIMSS item pool to the Ontario curriculum. *Studies in Educational Evaluation, 28*(1), 87–102.

Malagon, M. H., Rosenberg, M. B., & Winter, P. C. (2006). Developing aligned performance level descriptors for the English Language Development Assessment K–2 inventories. In *Aligning assessment to guide the learning of all students. State collaborative on assessment and student standards*: Washington, DC: Council of Chief State School Officers.

Manzo, K. K. Reading curricula don't make cut for federal review. *Education Week.* Retrieved August 15, 2007 from http://www.edweek.org/ew/articles/2007/08/15/01whatworks_web.h27.html?tmp=267034593

Maryland State Higher Education Commission. (2004). Report of the K–16 Workgroup: Highly Qualified Teacher Committee, Highly Qualified Administrator Committee, Standards and Curriculum Alignment Committee. *Maryland Partnership for Teaching and Learning in K–16.* Annapolis, MD: Maryland Higher Education Commission.

Marca, P. M., Redfield, D., & Winter, P. C. (2001). *Standards and state assessment systems: A guide to alignment.* Washington, DC: Council of Chief State School Officers.

McGehee, J. J., & Griffith, L. K. (2001). Large-scale assessments combined with curriculum alignment: Agents of change. *Theory into Practice, 40*(2), 137–144.

Moss-Mitchell, F. (1998). *The effects of curriculum alignment on the mathematics achievement of third-grade students as measured by the Iowa Test of Basic Skills: Implication for educational administrators.* Unpublished doctoral dissertation. Clark University, Atlanta, GA.

National Center for Education Statistics. (2007). *Mapping 2005 state proficiency standards onto the NAEP scales* (NCES 2007-482). U.S. Department of Education. Washington, DC: Author.

National Council of Teachers of Mathematics. (1989). *Curriculum and evaluation standards for school mathematics.* Reston, VA: Author.

National Research Council, (1996). *National Science Education Standards: Observe, interact, change, learn.* Washington, DC: Author.

Popham, J. W. (2001). *The truth about testing: An educator's call to action.* Alexandria, VA: Association for Supervision and Curriculum Development.

Porter, A. C., Kirst, M. W., Osthoff, E. J., Smithson, J. L., & Schneider, S, A, (1993). *Reform up close: An analysis of high school mathematics and science classrooms* (Final report to the National Science Foundation on Grant No. SAP-8953446 to the Consortium for Policy Research in Education). Madison, WI: Consortium for Policy Research in Education, University of Wisconsin-Madison.

Porter, A. C. (2002). Measuring content of instruction: Uses in research and practice. *Educational Researcher, 31*(7), 3–14.

Porter, A. C., Kirst, M. W., Osthoff, E., Smithson, J. L., & Schneider, S. (1994) *Reform of high school mathematics and science and opportunity to learn.* Consortium for Policy Research in Education Policy Briefs. New Brunswick, NJ: Rutgers University, Consortium for Policy Research in Education.

Porter, A. C., & Smithson J. L. (2001). *Defining, developing, and using curriculum indicators* (CPRE Research Report Series RR-048). Philadelphia: Consortium for Policy Research in Education, University of Pennsylvania.

Porter, A. C., & Smithson, J. L. (2002). *Alignment of assessments, standards, and instruction using curriculum indicator data.* Paper presented at National Council on Measurement in Education annual meeting New Orleans, LA.

Posner, G. J., & Rudnitsky, A. N. (2006). *Course design: A guide to curriculum development for teachers.* Boston: Pearson Education, Inc.

Price-Baugh, R. (1997). *Correlation of textbook alignment with student achievement scores.* Unpublished doctoral dissertation. Baylor University, Waco, TX.

Quellmalz, E., Kreikemeier, P., Haydel DeBarger, A., & Haertel, G. (March, 2006). *A Study of the Alignment of the NAEP, TIMSS, and New Standards Science Assessments with the inquiry abilities in the National Science Standards. Center for Technology in Learning, SRI International.* Paper presented at the American Educational Research Association, San Francisco, CA.

Rabinowitz, S., Roeber, E., Schroeder, S., & Sheinker, J. (January, 2006) *Creating aligned standards and assessment systems.* Washington, DC: Council of Chief State School Officers.

Reeves, D. B. (2006) *The learning leader: How to focus school improvement for better results.* Alexandria, VA: Association for Supervision and Curriculum Development.

Resnick, L. B., Rothman, R., Slattery, J. B., & Vranek, J. L. (2003). Benchmarking and Alignment of Standards and Testing. *Educational Assessment 9*(1&2), 1–27.

Robitaille, D. F., Schmidt, W. H., Raizen, S., McKnight C., Britton, E., & Nicol, C. (1993). *Curriculum frameworks for mathematics and science* (TIMSS Monograph No. 1). Vancouver, Canada: Pacific Educational Press.

Schmidt, W. H., McKnight, C. C., Houang, R. T., Wang, H. C., Wiley, D. E., Cogan, L. S., & Wolfe, R. G. (2001). *Why schools matter: A cross-national comparison of curriculum and learning.* San Francisco: Jossey-Bass.

Slavin, R. E., & Madden, N. A. (2003). *Success for all/Roots & wings: Summary of research on achievement outcomes. (Report no. 41 [revised]).* Baltimore, MD: Center for Research on the Education of Students Placed at Risk. Retrieved September, 2003 from http://www.successforall.net/_images/pdfs/SummaryofResearch-2003.pdf.

Squires, D. A. (1986, April). *Curriculum development with a mastery learning framework.* A paper presented at American Educational Research Association Annual Meeting, San Francisco, CA.

Squires, D. A. (2005a). *Aligning and balancing the standards-based curriculum.* Thousand Oaks, CA: Corwin Press.

Squires, D. A. (2005b) *The relationship between aligned curriculum and student achievement.* Charleston, WV: Edvantia, Inc.

Squires, D. A. (2005c) *Curriculum alignment: Literature review.* Charleston, WV: Appalachian Educational Lab.

Stallings, J., & Stipek, D. (1986). Research on early childhood and elementary teaching programs. In M. C. Wittrock (Ed.), *Handbook of research on teaching* (3rd ed., pp. 727–753). New York: Macmillan.

Stern, L., & Roseman, J. E. (2001). Textbook alignment. *Science Teacher 68*(7), 52–56.

Tallarico, I. (1984). *Effects of ecological factors on elementary school student performance on norm-referenced standardized tests: Non-reading behaviors.* Unpublished doctoral dissertation. University of San Francisco, CA.

Tindall, G. (2006). Alignment of alternate assessments using the Webb system. In *Aligning assessment to guide the learning of all students: Six reports. State collaborative on assessment and student standards*: Washington, DC: Council of Chief State School Officers.

Tomlinson, C. A., Kaplan, S. N., Renzulli, J. S., Purcell, J., Leppien, J., & Burns, D. (2002). *The parallel curriculum: A design to develop high potential and challenge high-ability learners.* Thousand Oaks, CA: Corwin Press.

Tyler, R. W. (1977). The organization of learning experiences. In A. A. Bellack & H. M. Kliebard (Eds.), *Curriculum and evaluation* (pp. 45–55). Berkeley, CA: McCutchan Publishing.

U.S. Department of Education. (2005). *Closing the achievement gap: Lessons from successful schools.* Washington, DC: Author.

Walberg, H. J. (1988, March). Synthesis of research on time and learning. *Educational Leadership,* pp. 76–84.

Webb, N. L. (January, 1997). *WISE Brief: Determining Alignment of Expectations and Assessments in Mathematics and Science Education* Retrieved February 22, 2006, from http://www.wcer.wisc.edu/archive/nise/Publications/Briefs/Vol_1_No_2/NISE_Brief_Vol_1_No_2.pdf].

Webb, N. L. (1999). *Alignment of science and mathematics standards and assessments in four states* (Research Monograph No. 18). Madison, WI: National Institute for Science Education and Council of Chief State School Officers.

Webb, N. L, Alt, M., Ely, R., Cormier, M., & Vesperman, B. (2006). The web alignment tool: Development, refinement, and dissemination. In *Aligning assessment to guide the learning of all students: Six reports. State Collaborative on Assessment and Student Standards:* Washington, DC: Council of Chief State School Officers.

Wiggins, G,. & McTighe, J. (2005). *Understanding by Design.* (2nd Ed.). Alexandria, VA: Association for Supervision and Curriculum Development.

Wise, L., & Alt, M. (2006). Assessing vertical alignment. In *Aligning assessment to guide the learning of all student: Six reports. State collaborative on assessment and student standards:* Washington, DC: Council of Chief State School Officers.

Wise, L.L., Zhang, L., Winter, P., Taylor, L., & Becke, D. E. (2006). Vertical alignment of grade-level expectations for student achievement: Report of a pilot study. In *Aligning assessment to guide the learning of all students. State collaborative on assessment and student standards:* Washington, DC: Council of Chief State School Officers.

Wishnick, K. T. (1989). *Relative effects on achievements scores of SES, gender, teacher effect and instructional alignment: A study of alignment's power in mastery learning.* Unpublished doctoral dissertation. University of San Francisco, CA.

Yager, R. E. (1983). The importance of terminology on teaching K–12 science. *Jounal of Research on Science Teaching, 20,* 577–588.

Index

The Corwin Press logo—a raven striding across an open book—represents the union of courage and learning. Corwin Press is committed to improving education for all learners by publishing books and other professional development resources for those serving the field of PreK–12 education. By providing practical, hands-on materials, Corwin Press continues to carry out the promise of its motto: **"Helping Educators Do Their Work Better."**